Love Life,
Live Life

About the Author

Sue Stone is a happiness and empowerment coach and business mentor. Her clientele range from private individuals to celebrities and city high-fliers. She is an international motivational and inspirational speaker and is available for talks, one-to-one sessions, seminars and workshops. She is regularly on TV and radio.

Also available: CD *The Power of Positive Living.*

For contact details or to book Sue please visit www.suestone.com.

Love Life,
Live Life

How to Have Happiness and Success
Beyond Your Wildest Expectations

SUE STONE

piatkus

PIATKUS

Published in Great Britain in 2010 by Piatkus
First published in Great Britain in 2007 by Hemmick Press

Copyright © 2007 and 2010 by Sue Stone

A CIP catalogue record for this book
is available from the British Library

ISBN 978-0-7499-5245-7

Typeset in Sabon by M Rules
Printed and bound in Great Britain by
Clays Ltd, St Ives plc

Papers used by Piatkus are natural, renewable and
recyclable products sourced from well-managed forests and certified
in accordance with the rules of the Forest Stewardship Council.

Piatkus
An imprint of
Little, Brown Book Group
100 Victoria Embankment
London EC4Y 0DY

An Hachette UK Company
www.hachette.co.uk

www.piatkus.co.uk

Contents

Acknowledgements

With so much love and thanks to my mum, Sheila, and my dad, Graham, for everything they did for me when they were on this Earth plane and for their ongoing love and guidance.

To my three wonderful children, Natalie, Richard and Nick. What can I say? You have been the most supportive, loving children a mother could ever ask for. I love you dearly and I am very proud of you.

To Sara and Steve Blincoe, my sister and brother-in-law, for recording my CDs and television appearances and your ongoing support.

To Richard and Kim, my brother and sister-in-law, for your support.

To all my amazing friends (even to the ones I don't see any more), thank you for the support you gave me when I needed it.

To Di Lewis for my photograph.

Thank you all.

CHAPTER I

The Worst Year of My Life

As I sit here, happy and relaxed, in my beautiful home, I am thinking, 'Wow, this "stuff" *really* works.'

When I think back to how terrified and fearful I was for the future, with that feeling of peace of mind and happiness seemingly gone for ever, or so I thought, I truly believe that if *I* can come through this then so can everyone else!

That desperate period in my life is long gone now. My children and I live a totally happy and abundant life in the wonderful sanctuary of our home, set in a few acres, with our horses, chickens, ducks and cat Mischief.

I think back to that dreadful time and can remember waking up each morning, after a night of 'sleep' from the pills that my doctor had prescribed me, and suddenly my reality would hit me in a split second and the physical pain of fear would run through me. It would have been an easy option to stay in bed and bury myself away from the world, but my three young children kept me going. They needed me and I knew I had to be there for them. As a mother, the instinct of survival is a tremendous motivator not to give up.

Natalie, my daughter who was then 12, and my identical twin boys, Richard and Nick who were 10, did their best to support me, but they had no idea what was really going on. In a recent television interview, Natalie told how her memories are of me being very tense and snappy, and how they tried so very hard to please me. The poor darlings, it brings tears to my eyes just thinking back and writing this, and contemplating how horrid it must have been for them. However, we always had lots of cuddles, which kept us all going. I think they were a great support for each other and remain very close now.

My 'annus horribilis'

If I am perfectly honest, I had not been truly happy for years. My marriage had not been the happy union I had dreamed of. My 'annus horribilis' was 1999. It truly was the worst year of my life, but in reality the feeling of happiness and inner peace had left me long before then.

To give you a brief history, my husband, 'Peter', and I were married in May 1984 and I loved him very much. We had been working together in our business as friends the year before and, much to our amazement, we found we had fallen in love. It was a great feeling, and he didn't wait too long to propose. I was over the moon!

We were fairly tight for money in those days as the business was new, and I remember one Sunday we had to go through the jar of change on the windowsill to buy something to eat. But it didn't seem to matter. I certainly don't remember being fearful or unhappy; we were in love and love conquered all!

As the years went by the business expanded and so did our family with the births of our three lovely children. As much as I loved being a mum, I was also very involved with the running of the business. It was very much a male-dominated business – plastic injection moulding – but as time went by my business skills emerged and at the age of 29 I was appointed managing director and chairman of the company.

Unfortunately Peter and I grew in different directions, as is the case with so many marriages. He was very negative when things weren't going so well and he found it much easier to bury his head and not deal with the issues facing us at that time.

We did have some really good years in business, but we also had some challenging times. In our personal lives, Peter and I were doing more and more things apart and there didn't seem to be any love left between us. In April 1997 we separated.

I always had the belief that once something went wrong, there would always be a run of other things that would go wrong – and that is exactly what happened. With the knowledge that I have now, I realise just how destructive and self-fulfilling that belief was.

From a financial angle, things seemed to go from bad to worse. Our overheads were high, we were losing sales and cash flow became very tight. We were not able to take much money out of the business for living expenses. It was a very difficult time but I had no idea how much scarier it was yet to become.

A year after splitting up with Peter, I met someone else who I am going to call 'Ray'. It was a blind date set up by friends and it was pretty much love at first sight for both of us. There started the most tumultuous relationship I have ever had in my life! It was one of those all-consuming loves that was the best and the worst all in one.

The relationship would run smoothly for a few months, then we would split up, then we would get back together again, then we would split up again and so it went on, each time exhausting me emotionally and tearing my heart to pieces. I can't deny it took my focus away from the business, although I did my best at the time to keep all the balls in the air.

The upshot of all of this was that in early 1999 money in the business ran so short that once the bills were paid there was not a penny left for us. Peter was living separately so we had two mortgages to pay and an enormous business loan at the bank that was secured against my home.

I remember vividly the awful dawning of how desperate things had become! Each day I would sit in my office juggling money between accounts, in a frantic attempt to try and keep everything afloat. I can still picture what I was wearing on one particular day when I calculated that we had hit our overdraft limit on every single account, not only business and personal but also our credit cards. And this state of affairs was to continue for some months.

I remember the wretched sick feeling that I had at the time. Coming to terms with the reality that I could not get my hands on any money at all was a deeply frightening prospect! Rather stupidly, it never crossed my mind that I could be entitled to state benefits.

Once again, I was back to scraping around for any loose change; however, this time it was utterly terrifying. We had enormous bills to pay and people constantly chasing me for money. I had three hungry children to feed and I was nursing another broken heart, due to yet another split from Ray. My car, which had been bought on finance, had to be sold and with little other choice I resorted to borrowing £250 from my sister Sara in order to buy any old banger that just about got me from A to B.

Peter predictably gave up. He buried himself away in his cloud of negativity and despondency, and left me to face everything alone. He walked away from all responsibility; the children, the business, the debts. He did not accept any personal responsibility for what was going on in our lives, and blamed everybody and everything else.

I was desperate and my close friends knew it. Many helped me in lots of ways, both financially and emotionally, and without them I would have been lost.

My lovely mum, who sadly died in February 2005, was housebound at this time with the crippling disease multiple sclerosis. She knew things weren't right as I was so snappy. I didn't feel I could tell her just how bad things were and what was really going on, as it would only cause her to lie, bound to her bed, worrying about her daughter. I thought I was pretty good at putting on a brave face to her and the outside world, but mothers know when things aren't right and she would insist on giving me money at times. I would leave her house thinking, 'Thank God I've got enough to feed the kids for another few days.'

This desperately unhappy period in my life seemed to go on and on, but in reality it can only have lasted a few months. I existed from one day to the next in a haze of fear and uncertainty. Once again my heart was aching; Ray and I had split up yet again.

I look back now and realise that there are many people who have been through far worse than me for much longer, but for me, at the time, it was living hell.

One particular day I only had £10 left, and I had no idea where the next few pounds were going to come from. There was not an ounce of food in the house or petrol in the car. I knew I had to put £5 worth of petrol in the car, and I spent a couple of pounds on sausages and potatoes for the kids' supper. I hate to admit it but the rest went on the cheapest bottle of wine for me. A few glasses of wine each night seemed a must at the time and helped dull the pain that I was living with day in, day out.

I had lived in my family home all my life and consequently felt very safe there. However, not only was I falling behind on my mortgage payments but the bank, who had funded the business loan, were also becoming increasingly alert to the fact that things were not improving. The repayments each month were enormous and could not be sustained. I found myself facing over a quarter of a million pounds worth of debt alone with three young children to support and no income! I was terrified.

I was acutely aware that if I didn't take control, and put the house on the market, the bank would take over and before I knew it I would have a repossession situation on my hands and I would lose absolutely everything! The children and I would be homeless.

I remember vividly the day in 1999 when the particulars of sale came through for me to approve. I broke down and sobbed all day. I could not believe my life had come to this; I was losing my family home, the one that I had grown up in and loved – the roof over my children's heads – everything I had.

This was the turning point for me. When I woke up the next day I thought to myself, if I carry on like this I *am* going to lose everything. The depths of despair and unhappiness were crippling, but deep down I felt I had to do something to help myself. This really could not be *it*! Surely?

I hated the feeling of being out of control and unhappy, and I longed for the carefree times as a child when I went about my everyday life with sweet naivety, bouncing happily through life. I thought those days had gone for ever.

A life-changing step

In my soul-searching at this eleventh hour, something told me to go to the local bookshop in Bournemouth and I headed for the self-help section. I had no idea what I was looking for. I found myself just standing there, blankly staring at the shelves and waiting until a book 'jumped' out at me, which I bought and took home.

My stress levels were so high at the time and with all the anxiety I really cannot remember which book it was, but nevertheless it set me off on the right path. I immediately felt better about myself as I was finally doing something constructive.

Through reading such material I came to understand that my mindset and perception of the dire circumstances I found myself in needed a radical change.

I was hooked! From then on I scoured shops, markets, car boot sales and friends' bookcases for any self-help and mind, body and soul books, and I read and I read and I read . . .

It was going to prove to be one of the most significant life-changing steps that I had ever taken. I learnt SO much. Many people read personal development books at different times in their lives, yet I hear so many tell me that while it's all good in theory they never get round to putting what they have read into practice.

And THIS is the difference. I made a conscious, decisive choice that I would implement what I was learning into every aspect of my daily life.

I became an intrigued observer of how, slowly but surely, my life was transforming. A wonderful feeling of inner peace consumed me. The happiness, which I thought had long gone, returned. It is absolutely true that once you get it right on the inside, it's amazing how life starts to flow beautifully on the outside. Your inner world very much reflects your outer results.

In the following chapters I will share with you all that I have learnt, in the hope that you too can enjoy a wonderful life of happiness and prosperity, and that all who read this book may also experience the magic of transformation.

CHAPTER 2

We CAN Create the Life We Desire

It didn't matter which book I picked up and read, whether it was a personal development book or a spiritual book, the message was always the same and what I learnt was *really* exciting!

I began to understand that there is much more to life than the everyday challenges that we all face. I learnt about the power of our thoughts and feelings, and about our conscious and subconscious minds and the universal laws that exist. I also learnt about the incredible power that is within every single one of us, and I have realised as time has gone by that only a few people have any understanding of this power and many of us have yet to develop and use it to its full potential.

In this chapter I am going to focus on examining the power of our thoughts, our conscious mind and our subconscious mind. Understanding and learning to consciously implement the power of our thoughts is a vital and necessary component to accomplishing and achieving our most sought-after dreams and goals.

Thoughts in action

Thought is literally the seed that shapes your external world. Think about this for a minute. Had Alexander Graham Bell not *thought* that he could invent a device that would allow you to pick up a solid object with numerous holes in each end, one that you could hear from and talk into, as well as transmit your voice thousands of miles in lightning-fast time, you wouldn't have the convenience of being able to pick up the telephone and talk to someone on the other side of the world.

If the Wright brothers hadn't *thought* that they could create a machine that would allow people to seemingly defy the law of gravity, we wouldn't know what it was like, or be able to board an aeroplane giving us the ability to travel from one side of the world to the other in a matter of hours.

These are just a couple of examples of how the power of thought has affected our world. Now, obviously these examples were not just thought into immediate existence. I mention them to express the importance of the power of thoughts, or, more specifically, a particular thought as the seed that began the process. But, had the seed never been planted, the harvest would not exist. Once the seed is planted, it *has* to be nurtured (acted upon) in order to reach full maturity.

Of course, people say to me that these inventors had great minds and a great education, so the best examples are really to be found in your personal life. This will begin to give you some deeper insight as to the power of thoughts in your own world. Stop and think for a moment about the different people in your life, namely your family, friends, colleagues and people you work with, etc. By listening to what they say, you can come pretty close to determining what their predominant thought patterns are and begin to develop a deeper understanding of how the power of thoughts fits in to each individual circumstance.

In thinking about each of them individually, do you know anyone who constantly communicates a lack of money? If you do, I'd be willing to risk my reputation on suggesting that they don't have enough. That is the power of thoughts in action. Do you know of anyone who continually talks negatively about a specific relationship that they are in? I can assure you that this relationship is lacking in some way and the more focus given to that negativity the more trouble the relationship finds itself in. That too is the power of thoughts in action. Now think about someone who constantly talks or worries about being ill: I'm sure you'll find that they are ill a great deal of the time. How about someone that you know who is positive and upbeat all the time? In the same respect, their experience in life will show it.

These are excellent examples of the power of thoughts in action.

I used to say to myself, 'OK, but are we thinking these things because that is the situation we are in?' But the more I read and understood, I realised that it was me that had to make a major shift in *my* thinking and that the reason I was in my awful situation was that I had attracted the situation in the first place! It was hard to take on board at first, but a lack of money or the fear of something going wrong was often in the back of my mind.

Thoughts manifesting outcomes

This isn't just based on spiritual writings and teachings. Science has also discovered and documented the power of thoughts in manifesting outcomes in the physical world starting back in 1926. You will find a more in-depth explanation of this in Chapter 4 when I look at quantum physics.

Although the majority of people believe they are thinking these thoughts because of their circumstances, this is not the case. That is only a perception of the truth. The 'real truth' is that those circumstances are being created because that is what they are thinking! The fact that they continually think about each of these occurrences is enough to allow the subconscious mind to begin the process of what it is designed to do. It absorbs the thought as truth, stores it, and begins the process that will actually cause it to happen in the physical world. When we then start speaking about our thoughts we are reinforcing those thoughts with our words and this actually speeds up the process of materialisation, i.e. it coming into 'being' as our reality.

I have been introduced to many people through the years who are obviously unaware of the creative power of thoughts, and who by their consistent words and actions continually bring about circumstances in their lives that are in complete opposition to what it is they claim that they want. This is another area where people fail to understand the power of thoughts. Many times, although they may consciously desire one outcome their predominant focus is placed on what they DON'T have or what they fear and as a result they experience more of what they DON'T want.

What is crucial to understand is this. If you choose to have an abundant, happy and harmonious life, your predominant thoughts need to be focused on and in harmony with what is desired and NOT what is lacking. The universal laws (see Chapter 3) that have existed since the beginning of time will make certain that that is precisely what is received.

Very simply, we are all living magnets that radiate thought energy and we invariably attract into our lives those people and those circumstances that harmonise with our predominant thoughts. If we wish to attract different people, different circumstances and different events, we have to change the content of our conscious thinking minds. We can dramatically improve the quality of our lives by taking control of our minds and manufacturing beliefs and expectations consistent with what we want to happen in the future.

> Remember, we are what we think we are
> and we become what we say.

When you establish the belief that something will happen, the vibrational frequency of the power of thought, more specifically the emotion that these thoughts create and ignite, will attract precisely what is believed. You understand this principle when you turn on your radio and deliberately tune your receiver to match a signal from a broadcasting tower. If you tune into 96.1FM you don't for a moment expect to hear music from 102.3FM, do you? No! You understand that radio vibrational frequencies must match, and this is exactly the same as thought vibrational frequencies. Thoughts are a living, vibrating mass of energy packets that are every bit as real and alive as you and I.

The universal law of attraction

Your whole existence, everything that is, and everything that you experience in your day-to-day life, is brought about by one or other of the universal laws and the one that I am referring to here is known as the universal law of attraction. It is also known by other names such as 'sowing and reaping' (in the Christian community), karma (Buddhist) or, as science refers to it, cause and effect. What you call it is immaterial. All are one and the same and act in exact accordance within our universe.

There are many people in our world today who would argue about which of these is correct. What they would find if they chose to delve deeper, eliminate judgemental thinking and investigate the reasoning behind each, is that they are all one and the same and that each of them is absolutely correct!

Our current and ancestral spiritual teachers, as well as the many great spiritual writings, clearly tell us that whatever it is we sow (or do) we will reap (receive) accordingly.

What does that have to do with the power of thoughts? The thought is what you are sowing. What you sow (or think), you reap!

In Buddhist teachings, the law of karma says: 'For every event that occurs (initial act) there will follow another event whose existence was caused by the first, and that this second event (the outcome) will be pleasant or unpleasant based on the skilfulness of (or the unskilfulness of) the act which caused it.' What does this have to do with the power of thoughts? The thought instigates the cause of the event.

Science states that: 'For every cause (action) there must be an equal or greater effect (outcome).' Again the thought acts as the 'cause'. The only difference between the three, Christians, Buddhists and scientists, is in their presentation or delivery and the perception of the hearer.

While many have heard these various truths, the majority only relate them to visible physical activity and fail to look deeply enough to develop the understanding that in order for a physical activity to happen, it must first begin as a thought (the cause).

The bottom line is this. Our thoughts are the initial unseen seeds that determine the outcomes that we will experience in the physical world. It is just as we plant a seed in the soil; if we plant an apple seed we would expect to grow (reap) an apple tree; if we plant wheat, we would expect to reap wheat. This simple universal principle is known to all; even a young child understands this.

With the above being true, why would it be any different with our thoughts? It isn't! And this is what I found so exciting; that we *really* do have the power within to create the life that we want for ourselves. By developing an understanding of this simple principle, we can then go to work on restructuring and implementing the power of our thoughts to create what we want in our lives.

Just as we would plant the apple seed and receive an apple tree, whatever thought seeds we release into the universe must bring back to us in a physical form exactly what we planted. In the same way that we would not expect an apple seed to produce an oak tree, we cannot expect the thought seeds that create doubt, fear, lack and limitation to produce a harvest of abundance and happiness in our life. By the same token, if we choose to plant thought seeds that create love, joy, peace and prosperity, we will experience (reap) the harvest of those seeds.

As with all these examples, the same principles are what determine our health and wellbeing. If our thoughts are constantly focused on health and wellbeing in our body, we will reap a harvest of health and wellbeing. If we are constantly focused on sickness and disease or a fear of such, the universe will return to us exactly what it is that we asked it for (consciously or unconsciously), a body full of sickness and disease (dis-ease).

It doesn't matter what the situation or circumstance, whether it be health, finances, relationships, etc., our thoughts are every bit as creative in health situations as they are with money matters. And they are equally as creative and powerful in our personal relationships as they are in every other part of our life.

> If you change your thoughts, you will
> change your world!

I changed my thoughts and I certainly changed my world, inside and out. In Chapter 5 I take you through the stages of my own personal journey of transformation.

Become aware of your thoughts

Before I go into more depth about subconscious mind power, an extremely useful starting point at this stage is to become aware of your thoughts. Here are a few suggestions to help you.

- Write a thought diary for a week. Be extremely honest with yourself and write down as many of your thoughts as you can: good and bad. After just a few days, you will start to see interesting patterns in your thinking habits and perhaps a clear picture of what you are attracting into your life.

- Try and eliminate negative thoughts. I know this is easier said than done, but do pay attention to your thoughts, observe them and analyse them. If you're constantly thinking about why you're not good enough or why you can't achieve something – change those thoughts. Think about why you *are* good enough and why you *can* achieve something. *Deliberately* plant good thoughts! Practise it and in time it becomes easier.

- Try focusing on what you DO want out of life rather than thinking about what you DON'T want. Spend time thinking about what you have got to be grateful for rather than dwelling on what isn't right in your life.

These are a few basic tips to get you started. As you progress through this book, you will learn all the tools and techniques that I have used to enable my life transformation. At times the information may appear to be slightly repetitive, but I feel it is important to understand the basics and how everything interconnects.

The conscious and the subconscious

Thoughts, as you know, take place in the mind. The mind is divisible into two major parts: the conscious and the subconscious. The subconscious mind 'covers' about 88 per cent of your mind; the other 12 per cent is covered by the conscious mind. The conscious mind deals with over 60,000 thoughts each day! It is the thinking, reasoning mind; the mind that chooses. For example, you choose what you are going to eat and which clothes you are going to put on. You make all your decisions with your conscious mind. You could say that the conscious mind is the master of the subconscious. However, surprisingly to most of us, it is the subconscious that has the real power.

Our subconscious mind is the mind that knows who you are when you wake up each day, without you having to consciously think about it! It keeps your heart functioning automatically, and the process of digestion, circulation and breathing are carried out by your subconscious mind through processes independent of your conscious control. The subconscious mind accepts what is impressed upon it by our thoughts or what we consciously believe. Quite simply, whatever our conscious mind believes and accepts, the subconscious mind takes as an instruction and proceeds to manifest that thought in our lives and brings it into our reality through universal law. It does not reason in the same way as your conscious mind.

The subconscious mind is like the soil, which accepts any kind of seed, good or bad. We've already discussed the theory of sowing and reaping, so think of a farmer with a field ready to plant. The decision on what to sow is like the conscious mind. The field on which the plant will grow is like the subconscious. Whatever the farmer decides to sow (conscious), the field will grow (subconscious). If the farmer sows grains of wheat, he will reap wheat in due course. Likewise, should the farmer sow rotten seed of any kind, the predictable harvest will reflect this and a damaged crop can be anticipated! This is how our minds work too.

The problem is that the subconscious mind does not differentiate between positive and negative thoughts. It will act on any command handed down by the conscious mind. If we sow negative thoughts in our minds, we will reap negative consequences in our lives. If we sow positive thoughts in our minds, we will reap positive rewards and successes instead.

One of my favourite books is *The Power of Your Subconscious Mind* by Dr Joseph Murphy and I like the way he explains it: 'Our conscious mind takes the photo and our subconscious mind is the darkroom within which we develop the images that are to be played out in real life.' I believe that understanding the subconscious mind as a photographic mechanism can remove the emotion and struggle from changing your life, because if it is simply a matter of replacing existing mental images with new positive ones, you begin to see the ease with which you can change.

Intensified vibrations

Let's take a slightly more in-depth look now at what happens to our thoughts and this creative ability. The thoughts that you think about the most (your predominant thoughts) are created by your conscious mind, which then creates an electrochemical reaction in the brain. These reactions (vibrations) open neuro pathways for the vibrations to travel through the brain. As they travel, they are activating additional brain cells, which create an intensified electrochemical reaction or vibration.

When the thought (vibration) is repeated, the brain then attaches an emotion to it, which further intensifies the vibration and even more brain cells are attracted to it. This intensified vibration is then sent to and absorbed into the incredibly sophisticated part of you, your subconscious mind, which stores and immediately begins to act upon the information received.

Your subconscious mind does not differentiate between right and wrong, true or false, good or bad. It only acts as a storage device and holds precisely what it is given. Based on the information received (frequency vibrations), it then goes to work to match those vibrations, based on their frequency, and joins with, or is attracted by, vibrations of an equal frequency (remember the example I gave earlier of radio vibrational frequency).

This is what creates and shapes your world or reality. This is why it is so important to become conscious of and clearly understand the power of your thoughts and to become consciously aware of what YOUR thoughts are attracting into your world.

Many of the things you do on a day-to-day basis, even unconsciously, have a dramatic effect on what is being stored in your subconscious mind. Reading the negativity of the daily news, consistently watching violent TV shows, absorbing negative input from friends, family, etc. all play a major role in what you are 'allowing' and as a result experiencing in your day-to-day life. As is now widely accepted, a prime example of the damage caused from negative conditioning can be seen in adults who were verbally put down in their childhood/formative years.

The power of the subconscious mind is at work continually. If you are aware of negative thoughts and influences that may be affecting your outcomes, you will want to begin to take actions that will change them.

It is extremely important that you are very careful and selective as to what you allow your conscious mind to absorb and establish as belief in the future. This is crucial if you are to reach the potential that you have been provided with and are quite capable of achieving.

There should be no such thing as average people. Your average results exist because you have average or self-limiting beliefs. So many people's lives are governed by their self-limiting beliefs and negative thought patterns. Science and psychology have isolated this as the one prime cause for success or failure in life. It is the hidden self-image that you have of yourself. It controls your mind, just as surely as your mind controls your heartbeat. Your success in anything will never be greater than the image you have of yourself.

Your self-image operates like the thermostat in your home in that once your image is set, your life is on course to produce the physical manifestation of the mental image you hold. Your self-image is your own conception of the sort of person you are. It determines what you believe you are able to accomplish. Your self-image was very likely unconsciously formed from past experiences: your successes and failures; your humiliations and triumphs. This image or opinion you have of yourself will determine how you interpret other people's reactions to you and will significantly affect your success in everything you are ever going to do.

However, so often we are unaware of what our subconscious beliefs are. I personally had to take a big step out and take a long hard look at what was going on in my life and why these negative outcomes were occurring.

Conditioned beliefs

We have conditioned beliefs about every area of our life. We have beliefs about money, relationships, other people, ourselves, our opportunities or lack of opportunities, our health, our bodies, even life itself. If our beliefs are faulty or limiting in any area of our life, then this will result in our subconscious acting upon the etheric web, the energy fields of reality to attract to us these faulty limiting patterns.

Beliefs exist on a subconscious level. Hopes, desires, wishes, goals and intentions all exist on a conscious level. We think of them with our conscious mind. But beliefs are different. They are deeper and more entrenched. They are submerged vortexes of energy that we have unconsciously allowed to take root within us. If they are empowering, helpful beliefs, such as 'I am a competent, talented person capable of great success, achievement and happiness', then this will be our unconscious resonance and with this as our core belief we will attract to ourselves situations that match this imprint. Our subconscious will work day and night to make this a reality.

However, if we have faulty and limiting beliefs, such as 'I am an unworthy person and nothing ever works out for me', this then becomes our inner resonance and our subconscious, which works with whatever resonance has been imprinted, regardless of what it is, will attract to us situations that match these images.

Dealing with fear

We now know that understanding how our mind works helps us to understand ourselves and our present situation. This brings me on to the topic of fear. How do we deal with fear when it happens to us?

Fear is the result of our mind becoming fixated on images of an undesirable situation that we 'fear' will happen to us in the future. The effects of this are very real and they have their consequences. It is not just an unpleasant experience to be ignored or accepted stoically. It is a very powerful force that those who are unaware of mind power often use against themselves. Fear is the mind projecting within itself images of what it does not want to happen. If this is not recognised and dealt with early on, it can and will find root within our consciousness. When this happens fear becomes a daily occurrence and if these thoughts are allowed to repeat themselves over and over again, they will eventually make an imprint on a subconscious level.

Once this happens the subconscious mind begins to attract the exact experiences we have been projecting and are afraid of. It sounds like mind power in reverse, but it is not. It is yet another example of how mind power works so effectively, even when we use it unwittingly against ourselves. A better analogy would be to say that it is like driving a car in reverse when we want to go forward. There is no point complaining, 'What is wrong with this car?' Instead ask yourself, 'Why do I have the car in reverse?' Likewise, when you are in the grips of fear ask yourself, 'Why am I projecting images in my mind of events that I don't want to happen?'

Professional coaches who prepare their athletes to win know all too well that when an athlete has a 'fear of losing', they have already lost. Unless they can change their 'fear of losing' to an 'expectation of winning', such athletes' chances of winning are slim to none.

Fear of failure, poverty, never getting ahead, never meeting someone to share your life with or fear of _____ (you fill in the blank) is almost always setting in motion the exact events we do not want. It is sowing the seeds for plants we do not want to reap. It is ludicrous, counterproductive and totally unnecessary!

Now let me make it clear that not all our day-to-day concerns are fears. Fear is something different. It is obsessive and dominates us in a way that is not rational. It far oversteps the boundaries of normal concerns and, if we are not careful, will find a secure abode in our mind, where it can grow and paralyse our thought process.

Never let a concern turn into a fear. Concerns are fine; fears are unacceptable. Be ruthless in eliminating fears before they take root.

I think it is plain to see that knowing and understanding what our subconscious imprints are is critically important if we wish to have a happy, successful, fulfilling life. Sometimes it is not easy at first to identify our own subconscious imprints, but noticing any repeating patterns of behaviour, reactions or events in our life can highlight these. Indeed, seeing an expert, such as a counsellor or a qualified hypnotherapist, for example, can help enormously.

Change your beliefs and you will change your world!

Remember, everything you think, do, say and believe is picked up by your subconscious mind. In order to get your subconscious mind to create the changes you want, you need to create a new way of living. From all the research I have done and put to the test, I have found there are several elements that make up this powerful new way of living that truly makes this 'stuff' work.

Here is a great analogy. You have ten people rowing your boat in life. Now you convince one of them to go in a certain direction, but the other nine are still rowing in the opposite direction. How long do you think it would take that boat to turn around? Never! You have to get all of your rowers working for you in the same direction.

To help you to do this I have put together what I

call Sue's *powerful mind team*! In the rest of this book I will cover what I consider to be the crucial members of the team.

You will certainly see some changes in your life as you start to incorporate all the members of the powerful mind team. By using the power of visualisation (Chapter 8), writing down your goals (Chapter 9) and repeating your affirmations (Chapter 10), you can achieve amazing results. The powerful mind team will allow you to change your beliefs, assumptions and opinions about the most important person in your life – YOU! Let's get your energy working in a singular and purposeful direction; let's get all your rowers in life rowing in the same direction!

Your subconscious will become engaged in a process that transforms you for ever. The process is invisible and doesn't have to take a long time. It just happens over time, as long as you put in the practice and the discipline and develop the understanding, trust and faith in these unwavering powers and principles.

Positive thinking

Positive thinking is one of the most important things you need to practise throughout your life. The only problem is that a lot of people think they know what

positive thinking is, but instead they are really prac-
tising 'wishful thinking'. Here's the difference.
Wishful thinking is saying something like, 'I know
that things will get better. I'm sure I'll get a better
job. Things will work out in the end. Eventually I'll
meet someone I really like. I just have to keep trying.
I'm bound to make more money – I just know it.'
These are all examples of wishful thinking!

Positive thinking is more than just something you
do when things go wrong or when you try to correct
a situation. Positive thinking is a way of living; it's a
practice, a technique that you need to incorporate
into your daily life if you have any intentions of
changing things or accomplishing your goals. You
can't suddenly start when things go wrong and then
stop when things get better. Positive thinking requires
you to get rid of all your negative thought patterns
and create a new belief system.

There are plenty of helpful books out there, but
you can't rely on just reading the book to do this for
you. Why? It is YOU who must train YOUR mind to
work differently. Learning the art of positive thinking
from a book would be like learning to play football,
golf or tennis from a book. You'll get some great
ideas – but you need to practise and train yourself. It
took a lot of consistent discipline to retrain my mind
and eliminate any negative thinking and beliefs, but
boy has it been worth it!

It is important to mention that deep-rooted emotional states of negative thinking need to be acknowledged and not suppressed or denied. For example, if you are feeling fearful or anxious, acknowledge those emotions for what they are (perception) and do not try to hide, suppress or fight them. Acknowledge them in your conscious mind, accept them and then let them go. For some powerful techniques on 'letting go' see Chapter 7. If you genuinely feel that your fears are taking over your life then I would strongly recommend that you seek professional advice as well as using the techniques I suggest in Chapter 7 that have worked so well for me.

Regarding the 'everyday' type of negative thinking, from experience I've found that many people struggle at the start to eliminate these negative thoughts. Different techniques work better for some than others, so now I'm going to give you some excellent techniques for eliminating negatives from your mind.

> Remember, it does take time and discipline
> to retrain your mind!

Each technique is separate and independent from the other. In fact, some of these techniques will seem contradictory, but each will be highly effective in dealing with negative thinking.

Cut it off

The first technique is called 'cut it off'. With this technique the instant you recognise that you are thinking a negative thought, you acknowledge it and you end it. You don't argue with it, you don't analyse it, you don't defend yourself against it; you simply cut it off. Some people say, 'Cancel!' The moment you recognise that you're thinking a negative thought, simply cut it off and insert a totally different thought into your mind. The key here is to recognise the moment that you're thinking a negative thought. So whenever you become aware of negative thinking, act immediately, cut it off and set a totally different thought into your mind.

Label it

The second technique is called 'label it'. As soon as you recognise that you are thinking a negative thought, instead of cutting it off as you did with the first technique, label it. You say to yourself, 'What is happening inside me now is that I am experiencing a negative thought.' That's all it is and you keep reminding yourself of that. You keep reminding yourself that 'It's only a negative thought. It's only a negative thought.'

I'm going to share an astounding truth with you now that will help you immensely in ridding yourself of negatives. I'm going to write it in bold letters and I would like you to read it over at least three times before you continue, so that it becomes imprinted into your mind. Here it is:

Negatives only have power over you if you react to them!

Go back and read it again. Continue to read this statement until you fully realise that it's only you reacting to negatives that gives them power. The minute you start worrying in this way, the minute you start reacting to the negative, the minute you start working yourself up about it and an emotion is attached to it, it's got you. But when you recognise that negatives only have power over you when you react to them, then you can simply choose not to react. Label it. Remind yourself that it is only a negative thought. And then move on to something else more positive. Don't get trapped into thinking about it. Dismiss it. Once again, negatives only have power over you if you react to them.

Exaggerate the thought

Now the third technique for eliminating negatives is to 'exaggerate the thought into all ridiculousness'.

The exaggeration technique is a great technique, but you must exaggerate it into absurdity. The key word here is ridiculousness. Let's say that you're a salesperson and you're out making your sales calls and suddenly the thought comes to you, 'Ah, what's the use, I'm not going to make another sale today.' And then you catch yourself and you say, 'Wait a second, that's a negative thought.' With the exaggeration technique, what you might then say is, 'That's right, I'm not going to make another sale today. In fact, I wouldn't be surprised if, when I visit this next company, as soon as I open the door people are going to be throwing buckets of water at me, and then they're going to release pit bull terriers and German shepherds and I'm going to be bitten and I'm going to be wet, and then this great big mechanical boxing glove will come out and it's going to smash me in the face. And then everybody is going to leap up on their desks and reveal this great big banner that says, "You fool, why did you come here? You're never going to make another sale!"' Keep carrying on like this, exaggerating it until your mind says, 'OK, enough, this is ridiculous.' You then find yourself laughing at the thought, and once you're laughing at the thought, you have robbed it of all its power.

Wouldn't it be great if, when we had negative thoughts, they came with warning signs reading: 'It's only a negative thought, you don't have to believe it if you don't want to.' But negatives don't come like that. They come disguised as apparently real problems, or quietly, slipping in when we're not paying attention. And if we're not aware of the fact that our mind is the great trickster, forever conjuring up negative thoughts, then we'll buy into every single destructive thought that occurs to us. But with techniques like these, we have ways of dealing with negatives. That's why they are so valuable.

Counteract the negative

The fourth technique is to counteract the negative with the exact opposite.

Whatever the negative is saying to you, you counteract it by thinking the exact opposite thought. When the negative thought comes to you, 'I'm not going to make another sale today', you counteract it with, 'I'm going to make several more sales today.' When the negative thought comes to you, 'I'm never going to get ahead financially', you counteract it with the exact opposite – 'I'm going to be tremendously successful financially.' When the thought comes to you, 'I'm never going to have a meaningful relationship', you counteract it with the

exact opposite – 'I'm going to have a fabulous relationship.'

You see, the mind can think only one thought at a
time. It might seem to you that you're thinking many
thoughts all at once, but what is actually happening is
you're thinking one thought after another one
thought, after another one thought and so on. So if
you take out the negative and put in the exact opposite, you are taking the power away from that
negative. Don't feed the beast!

This is often the exact opposite to what most
people do. Most people, when they have something
that they don't want to have happen to them, think
about it, worry about it, focus on it, unconsciously
give it power and eventually they manifest it.

(You will find other great techniques for eliminating negativity and fear in Chapter 8 on visualisation
and Chapter 10 on affirmations.)

Alpha brain waves

One of the most powerful times to reprogramme your
subconscious mind is when you are in an alpha brain
wave state. In case this is the first time that you've
heard the term, I should explain that alpha brain
waves are one of the four categories of the brain

frequencies. When your brain vibrates at 7–14 Hz, you are said to be in alpha. The alpha brain wave is the most mysterious brain wave, arousing the interest of many researchers in recent decades.

Have you ever experienced a 'light bulb' moment when you are lying in the bath? Or suddenly found a solution to a problem just before you sleep or when you are meditating?

If you observe carefully, you will realise that creative ideas always come to you when you are relaxed and this is the time when you are in alpha. When you are in alpha brain waves your creative powers flow faster, you can recall things better (such as where you left your keys), you can learn things faster and you absorb information faster.

Besides alpha brain waves, the other brain waves include beta, theta and delta. When you are in beta, you are conscious and alert. Too much beta frequency can make you feel stressed and breathless. When you are in theta, you are in a twilight state; you are not conscious. When you dream in your sleep, you are in theta. When you are in delta, you are sleeping. You are not aware of what's happening because you are in an unconscious state of mind.

Every day, your brain state moves from delta (sleeping) to beta (alert) and then from beta back to delta. In between, you will experience alpha and theta.

The simplified relationship between your brain waves and your state of consciousness can be summarised in the figure below:

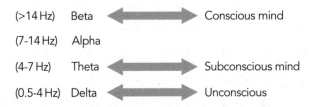

Alpha is the bridge between your conscious and your subconscious mind. One way to look at it is to imagine your mind is like a house with two rooms, separated by a door.

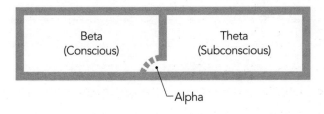

When you are in beta, you are in the conscious room. The door is closed so you have no access to the subconscious room. When you are in theta, you are in the subconscious room. The door is closed so you have no access to the conscious room. That's why most people can't remember exactly what they dream about. However, when you are in alpha, you are standing in the open doorway. You are conscious, yet you have access to your subconscious. This is why it is the best time to reprogramme your subconscious mind using techniques such as visualisation (Chapter 8) and affirmations (Chapter 10).

Finally, remember the really good news is that you DO have control over your thoughts. There are not many things in life that we do have complete control over, but our thoughts are one of those things. Your thoughts, once you learn to become conscious or aware of them, do not have control over you.

> Your thoughts do not think you,
> you think your thoughts!

CHAPTER 3

Universal Laws and Principles

The code for life on Earth

I have already talked about the power of our thoughts and the power of our subconscious mind and how all operate in conjunction with the universal laws. These laws, also referred to as spiritual laws or laws of nature, are the unwavering and unchanging principles that rule our entire universe and are the means by which our world continues to thrive and exist. Before I started on my quest to find happiness again, I had no idea of their existence, but once I had developed an awareness of how and why these incredible principles operate and aligned my thoughts and actions with what I wanted from life, I had amazing results. The key is in becoming aware of and applying these laws and principles.

Some people seem to think that you must be a 'religious fanatic' or a 'super-spiritual person' to allow the universal laws and principles to produce their desires and begin to make positive changes in their lives. This is absolutely not the case! The universal laws and principles that govern every aspect of existence and which are responsible for determining your life experience operate with precise, predictable and unwavering certainty and make no distinctions or judgements in how they operate or whom they work for.

These laws are inescapable and are at work 100 per cent of the time, regardless of your awareness or ignorance of them. Their operation makes no judgements or determinations based on your age, colour, creed, geographical location, education or gender, etc. The sun shines on all of us regardless. Just as electricity or gravity make no distinctions or judgements as to who they work for, universal laws operate within the same precise and unwavering fashion, and as a result through developing an awareness of how they work and aligning yourself with them you can begin to attract and experience outcomes, which many believe to be unreachable or impossible.

I know because I have done it! I have found life so much easier to live and I adopted a far more philosophical approach since I became aware of the universal laws. I love the way my friend Diana

Cooper, author of *A Little Light on the Spiritual Laws*, describes it in her book, 'If you drive on the roads without understanding the Highway Code you will have a confusing and difficult journey. When you learn and apply it your journey becomes safe and pleasant. There is also a code for life on Earth. Practise this at the highest level and you have the keys to heaven.'

The law of attraction

There are many universal laws but to keep to the purpose of my book, I am only going to touch on a few, in particular the law of attraction, the most powerful law of the universe.

A simple way of looking at this is to consider what happens when someone throws a ball into the air. It comes back down. Why? It has to, it's the law! Now, does it matter who threw that ball? No. Does it matter what their age is? No. Their education? No. Their background? No. Their faith or lack thereof? No. Nothing matters once they threw that ball, because as it leaves their fingertips, the universe and its principles take over, and that's the exact same thing that happens once you choose your thoughts!

So it is with the law of attraction. Whatever

thought energy (vibrating seed) you release into the universe, it creates and emits a specific vibratory pattern or frequency based on the type of thought. It is attracted by and joined with like energy of the same harmonious frequency or vibration that vibrates in resonance with it. This in turn creates the events or circumstances that you see manifest in your life every single day! You are literally attracting to yourself the thing that you have thought of (harvest). We are all familiar with the expression 'good vibes'.

In the same way, we attract people to us. People who do not resonate on our frequency simply are not attracted to us. They pass on by. The vibration you emit is made up of your conscious and unconscious energy, some of it repellent, some magnetic and some neutral. Quite simply, the underlying law is *like attracts like*.

Negative qualities such as neediness, desperation, greed, unkindness or thoughtlessness transmit on a low frequency. If we have elements of these in our nature, we will attract someone with similar energy into our life. Qualities such as love, kindness, happiness, gratitude or generosity transmit energy on a high frequency and also attract people with similar energy.

It is our underlying and often unconscious beliefs that attract situations and people to us. If you have a belief that you are not worthy, you will attract people into your life who mirror that belief back to you by treating you badly.

One of my girlfriends had a belief that men always let her down (sorry guys!), and of course that is exactly what she attracted into her life, men who let her down! Another friend believed that men always lie (once again, sorry guys, not my belief or personal experience at all) and yes, she had relationship after relationship with men who did lie to her. Of course the same happens in reverse, with men's beliefs. When these two girlfriends became aware of the impact their beliefs were having in their personal lives, they both worked very hard to change those beliefs, starting simply by looking around at other relationships and seeing that it was just not the case.

As I mentioned in Chapter 2, this is true in every area of our life; not just relationships but also health, money and so on.

Money is something that an awful lot of people want more of! Everyone who uses the law of attraction to attract and increase wealth and abundance will quickly learn that, in many ways, our emotions are linked closely with money.

Emotions can be both a strong benefit and a hindrance in your ability to attract financial abundance in your life. Your emotions determine the power or frequencies of your vibrations that are emitted to the universe. Focusing your emotions on the correct path will certainly boost your ability to attract greater financial wealth. But if the focus of your emotions is down the wrong path, it will block the abundance and prosperity that you want to attract.

So be aware how big vibrational differences can be. Your desire for an improvement in any financial situation cannot come to you if you feel jealous of your friends' or neighbours' good fortune, for the vibration of your desire and the vibration of your jealous feelings are differing and opposing vibrations.

In order to understand these workings, let's look at the two primary considerations when it comes to your emotions: money and the law of attraction.

Emotions that resist abundance

There are emotional states that can resist and obstruct abundance. Some of these commonly found states include fear, anger, uncertainty, hopelessness and desperation. If you want to attract money, but on the other hand worry whether you can handle all the wealth or whether it will ever truly come to you, you will subconsciously 'push' it away. If you need more money to pay your bills or fund your lifestyle, the fear of not having enough will subconsciously block it coming to you.

One of the biggest fallacies is to believe that money

will solve all of your problems. This is a sure-fire way to block off your abundance attraction because you have placed extreme importance on money, when actually it is not about money at all. Yes, money can and does make your life easier. But if your life was a mess to begin with, even when you have all the money you want it will still remain a mess.

Emotions that attract abundance

There are also emotional states that attract abundance all the time. Some of these abundance emotions include gratitude, passion, appreciation, joy, optimism and hopefulness. It is always good to start off with gratitude for what you have now before you start attracting more money into your life. Appreciate all the good in your life even if it appears not to be perfect and indeed you may genuinely feel there is little or nothing to be grateful for!

Every time something good happens, pause and be thankful for it. This will lead to a gradual increase in optimism for the future. This will increase your expectancy for good things in your life and you will begin to attract them. This cycle expands, as you will start to have an abundance of opportunities, enabling you to grow and develop personally.

This shift of your focus to these positive emotions

sends a new clear signal to the universe. When you combine this signal with clear, focused action steps, you will start to experience tangible abundance in your everyday life.

But like all good things, it may take time to see results. This is more likely if you have been focusing on the negative emotions for a long period of time. The hard part is being able to focus on these positive emotions even if the situation you are in is not what you wish for ... yet! This is so important because you must believe that things will change, even when nothing seems to be happening.

The problem is that most of the time you are not aware of the vibration you are offering. You are simply responding to things outside of you – current events, the news, how people treat you, the stock market, how much money you are making, how your children are doing at school, whether or not your favourite sports team wins – and this then creates a feeling that is either positive or negative.

Getting out of the vicious cycle

When you are simply responding unconsciously to what happens around you, you tend to stay 'stuck' in your current condition. This is why most people's lives never seem to change very much. They get stuck in a repeating cycle of recreating the same reality over and over by the vibration they are sending out.

> If you carry on doing what you've always done,
> you'll get more of what you've already got!

You don't have to be a victim of your lack of awareness of the law of attraction any more. It *is* possible to get out of this vicious cycle and create what you want instead of continually recreating what you already have. Here are some steps you can take so that you can begin immediately to break the cycle. (Of course, if you've been implementing the tips I gave you in Chapter 2 you will have already begun this process.)

Identify what you truly desire and eliminate the negative

In this first step towards breaking the cycle, it is important to focus on what you want rather than what you don't want by making effective affirmations (see Chapter 10 for a detailed look at affirmations, which are positive present-tense statements).

You must state what you want in the positive and

filter out the words 'don't', 'not' and 'no'. Remember, your mind works in pictures and if you say, 'I don't want to be angry', you are creating the picture and thus the vibration of being angry. You must create the opposite of what you don't want. For example, avoid statements such as, 'I don't want to be an angry and negative person' and instead replace them with more positively constructed statements, such as, 'I am a forgiving and positive person who is at peace with myself.'

We can't **solve problems** by using the same kind of **thinking** we used when we created them.

Albert Einstein

Raise your vibration level

Your job at step two is to create a vibrational match for that which you say you want to have. This means you must think about how would you be feeling if you already had those things – the perfect job, the perfect relationship, the amount of money that you want to have.

You need to identify what makes you feel good and think more of it and then learn not to tolerate your negative feelings. Take, say, 15 minutes each day to daydream about the things that make you feel good and really get your emotions involved by using all your senses. Try to imagine in full colour the sights, sounds, smell and feel of the people, places and objects that surround you in your perfect world.

Affirmations (which, as we have just seen, are positive present-tense statements) are an important component in raising your vibrational level to what it is you want. Remember, the law of attraction does not just respond to the words you use or the thoughts you think. It responds to how you feel about what you say and how you feel about what you think.

Release it and allow it

In this third step you simply release your affirmation, your vibration and your feelings to the universe to take care of your 'request', or 'order' as some call it. But you have to abstain from any doubts. If you doubt you can have what you want in any way, then you are not allowing it. You are pushing it away and you will end up with contradictory messages to the universe. I'll be covering this in more detail in later chapters.

History and research on the law of attraction

There is an incredible amount of recent scientific evidence available, including equations and experiments, which supports the truths of the law of attraction. By all means do your own research and come to your own conclusions. To help you, I have covered this area in more depth in Chapter 4 when I look at quantum physics.

Unlike the scientific evidence of the law of attraction, in the spiritual realm we only have certain teachings, writings and personal experiences to verify and support the truth of this amazing law. I cover some of my personal manifestation experiences in Chapter 5.

While scientists have made incredible breakthroughs in the past few hundred years with respect to understanding how events, conditions and circumstances in your life come into physical existence, our spiritual ancestors, as well as writers of numerous ancient texts, *knew* what science is only just coming to understand.

In fact, the great spiritual writings that have been uncovered, as well as the documented scripts of the greatest teachers in the history of the world, all talk about this phenomenon. Although the law of attraction may have only been given a name in recent years, it has existed since the beginning of time!

The law of polarity

The universal law of polarity is also found in the law of attraction. This law explains that everything in the universe has an equal and opposite counterpart. What often happens is that you may be experiencing something you don't think you asked for and definitely know you don't want. And yet, there it is. The truth is that you are always creating, but not always *consciously* creating.

As I explained in Chapter 2, the subconscious mind is the 'power centre' of your mind and is responsible for storing your memory, habits, personality, self-image and beliefs and it is in the subconscious that you have many intentions. Every intention you have is for your ultimate good. Unfortunately, just as it may be for your good, it may also show up in behaviours or situations that are on the other side of the coin. If you look closely at situations that have originally appeared to be negative, you may find that great opportunities were born from these situations. The law of polarity says that there are always two sides to every event – the positive and the negative. You can choose which you will focus your energy upon and thus create more of in your life – just as you can in the law of attraction.

At this point I want to touch briefly on a very emotive question that I get asked at times. If someone is born with a disability or a child becomes seriously ill at a very young age, people are naturally very defensive that they have not 'attracted' that into their lives. That same question used to bother me too, so I have done a lot of research on this now from both a spiritual and scientific viewpoint. From spiritual sources I have learnt and accept that before we are born we choose our sex, our parents, our brothers and sisters and what lessons we are going to learn in our lifetime. This also includes if we are to learn lessons from being disabled or terminally ill.

Scientific researchers have also backed up this information, in particular, Dr Helen Wambach, who wrote the book *Life Before Life*. Over a period of some years, she used hypnotic age regression on over a thousand people. Using hypnosis, she took them back to before they were born and 90 per cent recalled that their soul chose how they wanted to be born, the sex, parents, etc., and particularly the lessons and obstacles they were to overcome in their life.

I appreciate this is going to be hard for many people to take on board, especially when some

people experience the most difficult of circumstances, but if one can look at it as objectively as
possible, one can see that everything that happens in
life provides an opportunity to learn and grow for
your ultimate good.

The law of cause and effect

The universal law of cause and effect is the most
commonly felt and familiar law in the universe. It is
at the core of the law of attraction. For every cause
there is a reciprocating effect and for every effect
there is a preceding cause. Remember, our thoughts
are the causes and the conditions that we have are
the effects. To put it another way: you feel the effects
of what you create. It reminds you of the power that
you have in creating, and, naturally, being 'at cause'
of your world is far more powerful than being 'at
effect'.

The law of attraction says that you are the creator
of your experience by what you give your attention
to. This means that you are causing all the circumstances of your life, all the time (at some energetic
level – even if you cannot physically put your finger
on it). Choose what you want to focus your attention
on with consciousness and you will cause the effects
that you most desire.

The law of rhythm

The law of rhythm or 'going with the flow' has become somewhat of a catchphrase used to describe when you feel in alignment with whatever you are engaged in. The phrase 'going with the flow' is driven by the law of rhythm because it is your natural rhythm surfacing when you are feeling 'the flow'. Everything in the universe is moving in perfect rhythm and you have access to it when you let it in. When your body, mind and spirit are connecting, you experience the natural high of total alignment.

The law of attraction is all about being in alignment for 'focused creating' and an important requirement is letting it in.

CHAPTER 4

Understanding Quantum Physics

For those of you who wish to delve just a little bit further into the universal laws and principles that were introduced in the previous chapter, I'll endeavour here to explain quantum physics as simply and clearly as possible.

So, what is quantum physics?

Quantum physics is simply a science that studies and explains how everything in our world comes into existence. It starts from the physical aspect of the events, conditions and circumstances of everything in the universe, and breaks them down into their most basic form, while attempting to discover the source from where they are derived.

As I have already discussed throughout this book so far, quantum physics, spirituality, your thoughts, emotions and success in life or lack thereof are all closely intertwined or interconnected. In fact, as has been discovered by modern-day quantum physicists, they are much more interconnected than many had realised.

Unless you have already been exposed to physics at some point, just the mention of quantum physics may seem a bit overwhelming, but it's really not as intimidating or hard to understand as you may think. In fact, as you will soon discover, it is your thoughts and beliefs concerning quantum physics that make it easy or difficult to understand. If that statement seems a little puzzling at this point, rest assured it won't be once you've finished reading this chapter and develop a deeper understanding of how it is that quantum physics, or more specifically quantum mechanics, determines the outcomes in your life and the world around you.

Regardless of your current religious preference (or lack of it) and your level of scientific knowledge, these basic facts about quantum physics will enable you to construct the necessary solid foundation of 'awareness'. This will enable you to begin building and experiencing your life consciously and purposefully in a way that you desire.

I have found that familiarising myself with quantum physics has played a major role in enabling me to better understand how and why various 'growth lessons' that I experienced earlier in life really happened. They resulted in me developing a much deeper belief (or faith) in my own personal ability to begin consciously creating the events, conditions and circumstances that I desired.

Having begun my search for deeper meaning and understanding many years ago, seeking answers to some of the seemingly complex and unanswerable questions pertaining to life in general, I found answers in books that 'jumped' out at me. Through personal experiences and my reading, I discovered spirituality and finally quantum physics. I can assure you from a deep 'inner knowing' that both are intricately tied together and developing an understanding of them will arm you with an unshakeable faith capable of manifesting dramatic and, in many cases, seemingly miraculous life changes.

In fact I can safely say that quantum physics has proven to be the icing on the cake for me. It is one of the greatest and most important discoveries that I have ever made in relation to enhancing my overall awareness and belief, and which proved to greatly enhance all that I had gained during my spiritual quest.

So in the simplest terms, in the hope that a basic understanding of quantum physics will assist you in the same way, I will now explain to you what quantum physics has discovered. Through this new-found understanding I hope that you too can fully grasp and develop the awareness of the vitally important and crucial role that such discoveries play in relation to your life experience and the physical outcomes that happen as a result.

The basics of quantum physics

Although it is not necessary to have a deep understanding of quantum physics for our purposes, a basic understanding will assist you greatly in establishing the belief (faith) of how your life unfolds. As a result it will enable you to further develop your ability to improve the overall quality of your life quickly and dramatically.

By the end of this chapter I believe you will have developed a much deeper understanding of how discoveries made through quantum physics can and do play an enormous role in your life. It shapes each and every event, condition and circumstance that you experience in your personal life, whether physically, financially, emotionally or spiritually.

Quantum physics is the study of how, what and why everything that makes up the universe as well as everything in it, both the seen as well as the unseen, is derived. It is a detailed study of what is known as quantum mechanics, which determines how everything in the cosmos has come to exist, beginning at the atomic and sub-atomic levels. More simply put, it is an in-depth study of the building blocks of the universe. Basically quantum physics consists of analysing things that are experienced in life in various forms and tracing them back to where they originated and were derived from, which, as you will soon discover, is energy.

As almost everyone discovered at school, everything that you can see in the physical world is made up of molecules.

Quantum physics researchers went a few steps back from the molecular stage and took these tiny little wonders and broke them down even further. They developed the ability to study the various things that make them up, which are known as sub-atomic particles.

Here's a simple breakdown of matter, beginning with molecules . . .

A molecule is quite simply the smallest part of a substance. Taking salt as an example, you can have a molecule of salt, but if you break it down any further into atoms, it is no longer salt.

The next step down from a molecule is an atom. The next step down from an atom is the sub-atomic particle, which consists of photons, leptons, electrons, neutrons, quarks, etc.

At this point in time, the sub-atomic level is as far as quantum physics is able to go. Although there is much more to discover, this probably is all that you'll need to know to begin making dramatic changes in relation to your life experience. Correct application of what you are about to learn can enable you to achieve levels of limitless success, fulfilment and happiness in your life that so many have come to 'believe' to be out of reach.

The pioneers of quantum physics

First let's look at what a few of the pioneers of what would come to be known as quantum physics discovered . . .

Newton and Einstein

Two men made two amazing discoveries that raised world awareness of their individual ability to consciously and purposefully create their life experience.

In 1925 an incredible discovery was made.
$E=MC^2$: Energy = EVERYTHING

This huge and amazing formula was discovered by a scientist named Albert Einstein.

This new discovery would dramatically change the views of the scientific community and what was previously believed to be true in relation to what it is that makes up our world and, to that point, how humankind believed that all things came to be. This previous understanding was called Newtonian physics. Based on Newtonian physics it was believed that all things just happened.

Newtonian physics was Isaac Newton's theory based on the late 17th-century belief that the universe was made up of solid objects, which were attracted towards each other by gravity. This theory was extended in the 19th century to include the structures of atoms as being the fundamental building blocks of nature. According to Newtonian physics, it was believed that atoms and the sub-atomic particles, of which they consisted, were of a solid nature.

What Einstein's world-changing discovery proved was that these atoms and the sub-atomic particles that formed them were not solid at all but rather vibrating frequencies of pure energy that gave them the 'appearance' of being solid. Everything that exists in the entire cosmos, which is experienced through the five physical senses, from the infinitely large to the infinitely small, from the macroscopic to the microscopic, went far beyond just the theory of trillions of solid atoms being attracted together by way of gravity.

Einstein's discovery took the Newtonian physics theory a step further and determined that these atoms and everything that they joined together to form, consisted of various frequencies of rapidly vibrating energy. The sub-atomic particles from which they are made are also, at their core, comprised of this pure energy.

Without getting into all the specifics of how Einstein came up with this formula, here is a visual display of what the formula $E=MC^2$ looks like and how it breaks down from the infinitely large to the infinitely small.

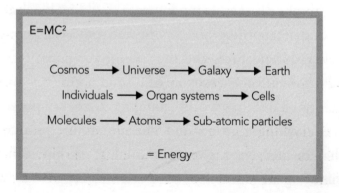

$E=MC^2$

Cosmos ⟶ Universe ⟶ Galaxy ⟶ Earth

Individuals ⟶ Organ systems ⟶ Cells

Molecules ⟶ Atoms ⟶ Sub-atomic particles

= Energy

Einstein's discovery proved that ALL things broken down to their most basic form consist of the same stuff. What is this stuff? This stuff is pure energy and it is this one energy that makes up ALL things.

It is interesting that with the amazing and potentially life-changing discoveries made as a result of quantum physics that the long outdated theory of Newtonian physics is still taught in many schools.

'One energy'

Without a basic understanding of quantum physics you might think that there are different forms of energy, such as energy that powers your home, energy that makes you get out of bed in the morning and keeps you going throughout the day, energy that fuels your car, etc. Although they appear, from a physical sense, to be varying types of energy at this level, due to varying structures and amounts of sub-atomic particles that comprise them, when analysed by quantum physicists and broken down into their purest form they, too, at their core, are all made up of this 'one energy'.

Everything that exists, whether nature, sound, colours, oxygen, the wind, thoughts, emotions, the chair you are sitting in, your car, your physical body, the stars, your dog, your ability to see, etc., exists only as a result of this very same energy.

To put it another way, ANYTHING and EVERYTHING that exists in the entire cosmos, when broken down and analysed into its purest form with sophisticated scientific tools and instruments, is merely a vibrating frequency of energy. This joins with energies of the same harmonious frequency to form what we 'perceive' and as a result experience in the physical world.

Now think about the implications here for just a minute. If ALL things in existence, at their core, are comprised of this same vibrating mass of pure energy, and I do mean ALL things, both the seen as well as the unseen, does that imply that we really are ALL ONE? The answer is 'Yes!'

Now if that has you feeling a little doubtful and uncomfortable at this point, I fully understand, but stay with me for a few more paragraphs and it will all begin to make perfect sense. This isn't something that I've concocted out of thin air. This is proven and documented science and the truth concerning it has been around for well over 80 years.

I still recall being approached by someone with this 'we are one' concept many years ago and I thought that person had lost the plot! My perception, as I have long since discovered, was made and based on a lack of awareness on my part as to how things truly work.

What I've found, as a result of many years of research and trial and error through personal experience, is that the person who initially shared this with me was absolutely 100 per cent correct!

My hope is that by sharing what I have discovered during this time with you, you will develop a deeper awareness based on my research and experiences, and as a result will not have to go through many of the 'growth lessons' that I and so many others have experienced.

Anyway, back to Einstein's discovery of $E=MC^2$ . . .

Although Einstein's history-making discovery was amazing enough in and of itself, it wouldn't be long before another, even more amazing discovery was made. When Einstein first discovered this truth he came to the conclusion that even though all things were derived as a result of this energy, which at that time was interpreted as being waves or as vibrating frequencies of energy, everything that happened as a result of them did so without any outside interference or participation. In other words he concluded that the events, conditions and circumstances, which happened in the universe, happened as a result of some unchangeable and immutable force. He believed that things just 'were the way they were' and that no one other than God, or whatever you perceive this 'force' to be, could change them.

Max Planck

As further scientific research and studies continued, differences of opinion arose. One of these differences came from a man named Max Planck, who believed that although Einstein's discovery was 'partially' correct, there was more to what Einstein had discovered that hadn't yet been revealed. How right he was!

Prior to Max Planck's research it was widely believed, based on Einstein's discovery, that energy travelled in waves and so that became the perceived reality of the scientific world. As technology advanced, more equipment became available that enabled scientists to analyse and experiment with these waves more closely, and as a result of this research a new discovery was made. The way that these sub-atomic particles behaved was influenced by the individual thoughts and beliefs of the scientist who was doing the observing. It wasn't until then that it was understood that these sub-atomic particles/waves (energy), which make up everything that we can see and experience, would literally change form into whatever the scientist who was studying it perceived and THOUGHT it to be!

In other words the energy being studied began taking form immediately, based on the thoughts and beliefs of the scientist who was observing it.

It's no wonder that Newton came up with his conclusion. Since he was the only one studying these atoms, and his belief at the time was in alignment with them being solid, they did indeed appear solid based on his 'belief' concerning what they were.

When Einstein, Planck and other scientists joined together their varying theories and opinions, they came to a conclusion regarding the truth about these atoms and, as a result, something even more amazing was discovered.

If a scientist studied them with the expectation (thought or belief) of seeing particles, particles were observed. If another scientist studied them with the expectation of seeing waves, then waves were observed. If they were studied with the expectation of first being seen as waves and then changing to particles or vice versa that is *exactly* what happened! The conclusion then was that this energy, these sub-atomic particles, acted and responded in exact proportion to the 'thoughts' and 'beliefs' that the scientist who was studying them had at that moment.

This discovery further proved to the scientists that anything and everything that exists in our world once existed as a wave (spiritual) and through individual observation and expectation was transformed into a particle (made physical), based only on what they THOUGHT and BELIEVED it would appear as!

The obvious conclusion from this amazing

sequence of events was that everyone's thoughts are also creative. In other words this energy, comprised of these sub-atomic particles, is directly affected and takes form based on the thoughts and beliefs of the person thinking them. As discovered in the laboratories, this observed energy acts in exact proportion to the way it is 'believed' that it will act and will provide the physical appearance based on the 'perception' of the thinker.

Now to take it even further, if that isn't amazing (and almost eerie) enough, something even more amazing was discovered by Max Planck, which has since been named quantum non-locality. Don't worry; it's much simpler than it sounds. What scientists discovered as a result is that these sub-atomic particles of energy, when broken in half (separated) in a laboratory setting, have the ability to communicate with each other and that communication is received immediately from one to the other, with zero regard to space and time as we know it, regardless of how far apart they may be.

Unlike our voices when we communicate, the sound of which takes time to travel, this communication (vibration) was received by one from the other at precisely the same time, regardless of how far away they are from each other.

In other words, this communication is not subject to time and space!

So what does this mean? It means that *everything* in the entire cosmos is nothing but a huge vibrating ball of interconnected infinite energy, which has the ability to communicate into infinity with no regard to space and time, and that what this energy joins together to form is based only on individual thought!

Quantum physics and you!

Now that you have a slightly deeper understanding of quantum physics, you are probably wondering what it all has to do with you. What can you hope to gain from it that will enable you to begin using it to experience abundance, happiness and success in your own life?

Just as the sub-atomic particles took whatever form the scientist studying them expected them to take based on their thoughts, so the events, conditions and circumstances that make up your reality take shape as you expect and believe they will!

To make it more personal and bring it closer to home, as quantum physics has shown, your thoughts and beliefs concerning any and every event, condition or circumstance, determine your life experience in the physical world.

We have already seen in Chapter 2 how your thoughts, which are determined by your beliefs, are broadcast outwards into the infinite field of energy much like a radio frequency, transformed from waves (spiritual realm) to particles (matter) and link together with additional energies that vibrate at a harmonious frequency and join together to shape what you come to see as your life experience in the physical world. *Your* physical world. You quite literally have the ability to mould and shape the various areas of your life, based on how you think, believe and feel!

That is how our world was created to operate. Regardless of what you may currently believe to be true, you are NOT the victim of some capricious set of circumstances. You are quite literally the creator of your own reality! You are the artist that paints the picture. You are the producer and director of your movie. If you want to change the scene on the canvas, you only need to use a different brush. If you don't like the scenes that are being played out in your movie you only need to change the script, which is responsible for creating them. If you desire to change the events, conditions and circumstances in your life you only need to change the thoughts, beliefs and emotions that are responsible for bringing them into and making them your reality.

In a nutshell, whatever you think about and believe to be true, regardless if those beliefs are based on 'real truth' or 'perceived truth', determines how your life will unfold.

Quantum physics tells us that it is the act of observing an object (events, conditions and circumstances) that causes it to be there and the outcome is based only on how we observe it. An object cannot and does not exist independently of its observer!

If you believe at some level, whether consciously or unconsciously, that money is difficult to come by, the energy emitted and broadcast will harmonise with energy of a harmonious frequency and your life will reflect that of money being difficult to come by.

By the same token, if you believe that money flows to you effortlessly and maintain the conscious and subconscious beliefs regarding that, you will find that money becomes easy to acquire.

As quantum physics has proven, you are responsible for whatever outcomes you are experiencing in your life. It *really* is that simple.

Put it to the test

OK, we've covered a lot of ground in this chapter and although your head may be spinning and emotions running high, I encourage you to attempt to disprove what we have covered here. You don't have to take my word for it . . . I want you to test it for yourself. I would much rather that you find out for yourself through your own due diligence and put what you find to work to begin changing your life experiences from this point, if you should choose to do so.

For some, this understanding of quantum physics combined with the spiritual principles of life will be enough to grasp the correlation between what quantum physics has discovered and what the greatest and wisest teachers in the history of the world have taught for thousands and thousands of years.

Now, having an understanding of the basics of quantum physics and quantum mechanics, all that you need to do to implement them into your life is to, first of all, develop the belief that it's all true (and it is). Secondly, begin to 'consciously' put it to work in your own life and you will become empowered to change those events, conditions and circumstances that you currently find to be unpleasant.

Regardless of how deeply you may search you will find that it is 100 per cent accurate 100 per cent of the time WITHOUT FAIL, and that your life experiences happen as a result of how you think and believe they will, whether at a conscious or subconscious level.

For those who may have a religious background, you will discover if you choose to delve deeply enough that what has been discovered by modern-day science is precisely what the great spiritual teachers of the world have shared and attempted to get their followers to understand for thousands upon thousands of years.

The conclusions that have been arrived at thus far through the study of quantum physics align perfectly with what all the major religions of the world have always taught in some form.

You have been provided with the inalienable right of free will and been given the ability to choose what you will do in your life. You can choose to investigate quantum physics, delve more deeply into what has been shared here and discover it as a truth for yourself or continue to create your life unconsciously. You can choose to remain a victim of circumstance or align your actions (thoughts and beliefs) with the greatest creative force in the universe and become a conscious creator of circumstance.

That is a choice only you can make. You and you alone are responsible for the events, conditions and circumstances that make up your life. Of course, whether or not you choose to accept it is also your decision.

Please note that there are still many different interpretations of quantum theory and what is for certain is that we will learn much more in the coming decades about the mechanics of how we create our own reality. The fact that we are able to do it, however, is proven beyond doubt.

CHAPTER 5

My Journey of Transformation

The more I read the more I started to believe that there was something very powerful in the message I was getting.

I'd learnt how powerful our thoughts are, both positive and negative, and that too many people think about and visualise what they DON'T want to happen. That was exactly what I was doing. The negative, fearful thoughts I was experiencing about my situation were only going to attract more of what I didn't want in my life. I was terrified about my future and I spent most of my time thinking how I was going to get enough money together to feed the kids, how I was going to cope with the next call chasing me for money, on top of worrying about being homeless. My partner Ray was not in my life and at the time I thought I could never be happy again without him!

I have frequently been asked how I started to turn my life around, what it was that I did to change the pattern.

The answer is simple. I made an effort to become consciously aware of the thoughts that I was thinking.

I became the observer of my thoughts. I also took a long hard look at myself and where I was in my life and potentially where I was heading, through the power of my own thought process.

I realised that something had to be done, quickly! What I did was not difficult but it does require consistency and discipline. Here's how I did it.

Replace negative thoughts with something positive

I literally took systematic, purposeful control of the thoughts that I allowed to stay in my head. The aim was to eliminate all negative thoughts. Easier said than done I know!

It was important to replace the negative thought with something positive. At the time I was so desperate that it was a struggle to think of anything positive.

But one thing was for sure; I knew that I wanted to be happy again.

Remember, think about what you DO want out of life, and don't think about and dwell on what you DON'T want.

Focus on the desired end result

From everything I had learnt I realised how important it was to visualise and focus on my desired end result. So after banishing any negative thought, I would always immediately replace it with a picture in my mind of the children and I happy and laughing together, feeling really good about ourselves and living in a wonderful home, wherever that may be! Even though I hadn't got a clue what was going to make me happy or where this lovely home was, I figured that if I was feeling really good and at peace with myself, life must be going well for me.

I cannot reiterate too often how important it is to visualise the desired *end* result, your actual goal, whether it be happiness and inner peace (which I now believe to be the most important core element), or a new job, a new house, a loving partner, etc.

Literally, imagine yourself already in that desired situation.

Do not spend time worrying about how you will achieve your goal. The key is to trust that the unwavering powers of the universal laws will bring into your life those circumstances, situations, events or people to enable you or give you the opportunity to achieve your desires. For more comprehensive techniques to help you achieve these desires see Chapters 8 and 9 on visualisation and goal setting.

Every time I had a dip or a wobble (and I had plenty of them in those days, believe me!), I would think of a great phrase my lovely friend Meryl used that helped me so much. That key phrase was 'our thoughts create our future', and every time I found myself having a negative, fearful thought, I knew that was not the future I desired and I banished that thought from my mind. I would imagine myself physically pulling that negative thought out, as if it were an unwanted old tissue and throwing it as far away as possible and immediately would visualise my children and I totally happy in our wonderful new home.

I had also learnt about the magnetic force of our feelings, that if we were feeling low or unhappy, we would attract more on that low negative vibration. To enable myself to feel better I would focus on all that I had to be grateful for, which at the time did not seem very much, but my health, family and friends have always been very important to me, and I felt lucky to have them. I tried very hard to do something that would cheer me up and help me focus on the positive things around me.

Every spare moment throughout the day I concentrated on my affirmations (remember, these are repeated positive present-tense statements), visualisations and goals, and I continued to read positive, uplifting personal development and spiritual books, which reaffirmed this way of living.

Very gradually things started to look brighter. Slowly but surely nice things started happening to me, which I always acknowledged and thanked the universe for.

I started to have a much clearer head about the way forward with the business. If I was unsure about making a decision I had learnt to do nothing, rather than make a hasty one borne out of fear. I trusted that the right path would become apparent to me and it always did. Doing something constructive to help the situation made me feel better and of course as the positives started flowing, in accordance with what I had been visualising, so did my trust and belief. The business improved and consequently so did my income!

As I have written, my main overriding goal and visualisation was one of happiness in our new wonderful home. I kept this up each and every day, even though the months ticked by and the estate agents were bringing people around to view my house. I had to go out; I couldn't bear to see it all going on. I still had no real idea of where we were going to live, but consistently kept working on myself by eliminating negative thoughts, focusing on my positive thoughts and desires, together with all the other new techniques I had learnt.

My inner world was becoming calmer and this was beginning to be reflected in my outer world. I still couldn't say that I was happy, but I was certainly more at peace with myself and life in general.

As my financial position started to improve, I viewed several properties that were on the market, but to be honest found it all pretty depressing. I never gave up hope though or lost that vision and feeling that I *would* find our sanctuary of a home.

Finally I had a buyer for my house and it was all systems go! One sunny day in early spring 2000 I bumped into an old friend who was an estate agent. He told me about a house for sale that had just been reduced in price and it was located in a lane that I had wanted to live in since childhood. I decided it was too much money, but thought I would have a look around out of curiosity.

Well, I walked into the house, looked out into the garden and thought, 'Wow, this is it! I have got to live here.' At the same time, I had such a strong gut feeling and I 'knew' that I would somehow make this happen.

My visualisations intensified, as I was now able to picture exactly the property I wanted. In addition, there were three affirmations I chanted regularly each day.

> *I trust in the power and the magic of the*
> *universe.*
> *I believe in miracles; miracles happen to me.*
> *I have more love, happiness and abundance*
> *in my life than I ever imagined possible.*

One year on from my most desperate times the children and I moved into our beautiful home, Chimneys. I met all the right people at just the right time and I received the help and guidance needed for me to achieve my dream. Business contracts poured in and friends helped top up the shortfall on the house purchase price.

All this amazed many people and they saw it as quite courageous and incredible. But please note this took one year and not just a few weeks to achieve. It is so important to consistently work on yourself in every way and don't give up! It takes time to become the deliberate creator of your reality, so don't be disheartened if you don't see the results as quickly as you would like.

Every day I walked round the house and the garden and the gratitude I felt was overwhelming. Being grateful and appreciative is such a powerful emotion for attracting more and more into your life to be grateful for.

Unfortunately life was going in the opposite direction for Peter, my ex-husband. He was totally consumed by his negativity, buried his head and kept saying, 'This is the end' and slowly but surely he attracted more on that negative vibration. He lost his car and his home. I was able to give him my old banger as I had bought a slightly better, more reliable car and his mother opened up her home for him.

Peter's dreadful period unfortunately lasted for several years. He could not get his head around what I had achieved and where the children and I were living. I tried so hard to encourage him along the same path of 'positive living', but I have now learnt that you can hand someone all the tools but if they are not ready or prepared to pick them up, you cannot make them do it. In more recent years, however, he has made a conscious effort to work on himself and I am pleased to say that he is far happier, positive and upbeat and achieving amazing things in his life. In fact the two of us get along brilliantly well now and have a fantastic friendship.

I believe it takes more courage to address and face your problems, whether financial or personal, than to bury your head, which is by far the easier option in the short term. Long term, however, it is disastrous.

I had to find so much courage within me to make

the changes that occurred in our lives and one of those times was before the house sale went through. Peter's lack of action and negativity had resulted in me getting left with all the debts, including the very large secured business loan. The bank had intended to take all the proceeds from the sale of the house to repay this loan, but once I had found our dream home I was determined to live there.

My local bank manager thought I was wasting my time, but, undeterred, I got some facts and figures together and went to the top! I was dealing with the recovery section of the bank by now. I put my case forward and asked them to give me a year to repay the debt. This took a lot of 'balls' I can tell you.

Waiting for their response was nerve-wracking, but when the call came in one week later to tell me that they were prepared to go with my proposal, I put the telephone down, screamed hysterically with excitement and danced for joy in the kitchen.

Looking back, that year seemed to go very quickly, but my visualisation powers and manifestation skills were improving quickly too! I managed to raise most of the necessary funds, but Ray, who at that time was back in my life, thankfully helped with the shortfall.

My relationship with Ray brought me into contact with a lady called Diane Egby-Edwards, a very significant 'teacher' along my journey. She is a trained hypnotherapist, sound healer and emotional freedom technique (EFT) practitioner.

I met her a year after I had moved into Chimneys. How our meeting came about was quite amazing. Despite a period of calm together, unfortunately I took what I considered to be the final emotional knock from Ray. I felt devastated and I thought, 'Right that's it; I have got to get him out of my life.'

In my desperation I had decided that I wanted to be hypnotised to help me forget about him! It seems terribly naive to me now as I write this, but that was how I felt at that time and I prayed it would actually work. I picked up the *Yellow Pages*, went to the 'Hypnotherapist' section and there were pages and pages of them. I flicked through. One name jumped out at me and that was Diane. I tried calling but the answerphone came on so I just put the phone down.

I went away early the next day for a week and I asked my great friend Mandy if there was one thing she could do for me while I was away. Her great mission was to get me an appointment with a hypnotherapist for the Monday I was back. Mandy called the following Sunday and said that she had found me someone. She had opened the *Yellow Pages* and said out loud, 'Please show me the right person to help Sue.' Guess what? The name that came up was Diane Egby-Edwards! Mandy had no idea that I had looked in the *Yellow Pages* myself and that I had already tried to call Diane! We both found that quite 'spooky' at the time, but felt that she must be the right person for me and indeed she proved herself to be so.

I went to see Diane and she started talking to me about unconditional love, living in the 'now' and letting go of the past. For a while I couldn't really get my head around what she was talking about, but as she explained further, things did start to make sense. She used some incredible techniques to help me dissolve the pain that I was feeling, but of course to hypnotise me to forget about Ray was impossible. I understood the importance of letting go of the past and living in the present. Now and over the weeks I continued to work on myself with the various techniques she had shown me, along with others I had read about.

And what a difference it made! Life started getting better and better, and I really could not believe how fantastic I felt inside and out.

The importance of letting go and the various tried and tested techniques I learnt are included in Chapter 7.

The biggest and most significant breakthrough for me was when I realised that it just did not matter whether I ever saw Ray again! I still loved him but felt at peace and happy with this thought. Having been desperately fearful that I would never be happy without him in my life, this was a major leap forward.

I promise you that I have never looked back! I hate to think what I must have been like, but so many people over the years have remarked on my amazing transformation and have said that they want 'a bit of what I've got!'

As the years have gone by I have managed to develop a purely positive focused energy. It takes time and it takes practice, but when you crack it, it is fantastic! Whatever I focus on manifests in my life; it is truly amazing.

Positive manifestations

I am going to share with you now a few of my manifestation stories. These will demonstrate how subtle some of the signs are when we attract the right opportunities into our lives and how important it is to act upon them.

We have a few acres of land at Chimneys and when we first moved in my children and I discussed how lovely it would be to have a horse one day. Some four years later, I felt the time was right.

I put into practice all the manifestation skills I had learnt and refined, carried out my affirmations, goal setting and visualisations to send out the right energy into the universe. I visualised a beautiful horse with a lovely temperament, quite big, in my back garden and trusted the right one would come along.

Just a month later my sons and I were walking in our lane when we bumped into a lady who kept her horse nearby. I had seen her several times and many of the other 'horsey' people in the lane, but in all of the four years at Chimneys we had never met or spoken to any of them. The opportunity had simply never arisen.

Suddenly, there she was in front of me and we started talking. During the conversation I told her that I was looking for a horse. Coming home from our walk, I remember feeling it was very significant that we had spoken to this lady. I never had 'horsey' chats with people and within a few weeks of sending the thought energy out we were meeting 'horsey' people!

Two weeks later we had a knock at the door. It was the same lady with a piece of paper in her hand with a name and telephone number. She had just heard of another lady who had recently moved into the area, who kept her horse in our lane, and that for a number of personal reasons she was unable to look after it any more. Was I interested?

Of course I immediately acted upon the opportunity and called the number. We arranged to meet a few hours later and to my delight there in front of me was a beautiful horse, 16.1 hands high (just the size I wanted and had visualised) and clearly she had a lovely temperament.

I couldn't believe it! Even better still, her owner didn't want any money for her as long as she could come and see her whenever she liked. Mei Mei has now lived with us for the last three years and has been a great source of pleasure.

Six months after Mei Mei joined us, we thought it would be great to have a second horse to ride and to give her some company. My split-second reaction was to think that I could never pull off the same result again, but decided that was far too negative!

I banished that self-limiting thought from my mind and worked on all my manifesting techniques. It took just one and a half days this time before I was connected to the owner of another beautiful horse, also 16.1 hands high, called Alabama, who also now lives with us. Two stunning horses in our back garden, what a gift from the universe!

Another story I like to tell is the one of my car. As you will have read in Chapter 1, when things got desperate I sold the car I had and bought an old banger for £250 and purchased a slightly better car several months later. However, I had always loved BMW convertibles, especially those in a particularly pretty blue with cream leather interior. To own one myself was one of my goals, but that was totally out of reach for me financially at the time.

By now I was really getting into this manifestation lark, so what did I do? I wrote my goal down and visualised the kids and I driving around in our pretty blue BMW convertible, roof down, wind blowing through our hair and the four of us laughing and having fun together.

> Visualise and create the emotion of success as if you have already achieved your goal.

I did this *every* day, along with the other goals and visualisations I had. This particular goal took one year to achieve – remember, persistence and trust is crucial – and slowly but surely my financial situation improved enough to enable me to buy the car of my dreams. One Saturday I woke up and out the blue I had this 'knowing' or flash of inspiration that we should go 'car shopping' that day.

Having learnt to trust and recognise my 'knowings', we changed our previous plans for the day. Richard and Nick, my twin sons, came with me and we drove straight to the local BMW dealers. Sitting on the forecourt was a BMW convertible at just the price I had budgeted for, in the exact pretty blue I had wanted with cream leather interior!

We did the deal that day. It was the height of the

summer and if I had not listened to that flash of inspiration and acted upon it, someone else would have bought my car!

On a more pragmatic level, in February 2006 I decided it was time to let go of the business and concentrate all my efforts on helping others transform their lives, as I had done. I had lost interest in the business a few years before and wanted to pursue my passion.

I wrote down my goal with a date by which I intended to achieve it, 31 May that year. It ought to have been a tall order, but it felt right to me. As always I visualised daily the end result – the final signing of the contract and celebrating the sale of the business, drinking champagne with my family and friends.

Twelve days later I was on the telephone to one of our customers, when suddenly something told me to ask him if he would be interested in buying my business. It came from nowhere, but by now totally trusting what I am given, I did exactly that and asked him who his boss was and did he think he would be interested. Within 10 minutes the boss called back and said he was very interested.

As it turned out I did not sell the business to him, but what that conversation did was focus my mind on putting a 'sales pack' together, which prior to that I had not done and was clearly necessary.

My common-sense head had calculated that I

would get more money from another company not already in the same market place and who would value the new customer database.

This inspired me to search on the internet and one company 'jumped' out at me. I telephoned them immediately and the managing director told me that I could not have called at a better time! They had just moved into a very large factory, had a lot of spare capacity and were looking for new products to manufacture. I agreed to go and see him the next day.

Two meetings later and contracts were drawn up. Guess what day *he* chose to complete the sale on? Yes, 31 May 2006! And of course that evening I was drinking champagne with my family and friends.

These are just a few of my personal stories of manifestation to date. I experience so many on a daily basis and it is important to recognise and appreciate each one, however small. The universe is at work all the time and without awareness it is easy to overlook or miss them.

My latest goal

For the record I am going to put in print my latest goal; to live in a house that previously I would have felt was way beyond my wildest dreams. To have this house as our home is an incredible leap from where we are now, but from all the research I have done over the years, I have learnt that if you can manifest at *one* level you can manifest at *any* level.

Having seen the house in a glossy magazine, I decided to see just how powerful and unlimited this manifestation process can be. Even with my personal evidence and testimonies to date, me being me, I really want to test it to the limit.

This house is beautiful and will make a wonderful sanctuary for me to do my work and fulfil my passion to help others.

To give you a flavour, it is set in the New Forest within 44 acres of landscaped gardens with lakes and woodland . . . Do you get the feel?

I suspect that some people who know me think that I've lost the plot! A couple of friends said it sounds like their worst nightmare having somewhere so big, but to me it feels great. I have been round the house three times now and it feels like home already!

I am not there yet, but watch this space. This is going to be one hell of a manifestation! My next book will tell the story, once it has become my reality.

Acknowledging that these material and physical manifestations are fantastic, in truth, the most empowering state of 'being' is to be at peace with oneself and to experience happiness and joy. It truly does become a way of living once you think about and 'see' life from a different perspective.

It may have taken me some 40 years, but now I understand the importance of being completely at peace and at one with yourself, despite what is going on in your external world.

How empowering that state of 'being' is. I never, ever thought I would feel the way that I do and have done so for some years now. I live and thrive on each and every day for what it brings. I still get challenges at times, as do we all, but it is how we view and think about our 'problems' that can make them appear too big to manage and make us unhappy.

People, more often than not, think that what they want is money, relationships and material possessions, but what they truly want is happiness. Wealth, health and relationships are simply the rewards of being happy.

Happiness and inner peace is a state of vibration that is in harmony with the universe. As I have said earlier, the same frequency vibrations tend to attract each other, therefore, the vibration of happiness is going to attract more happiness, wealth, better relationships and improved health. If money is your primary goal, you may not get it and be disappointed, but if you desire happiness, money will flow to you.

How many of us are unaware of this simple yet profound truth.

Remember, you *do* have a choice and you *do* have free will, whether or not you are aware of this. If you really want to change your life the first positive step is to make the choice to help yourself and hold the belief that you can. Reading this book is, in itself, a very positive first step, and I really hope the information contained within it will help you as much as it has helped me.

Wise words

To conclude this chapter, look at these wise words from the American personal development guru Jim Rohn (www.jimrohn.com).

What we ponder and what we think about sets the course of our life. Any day we wish, we can discipline ourselves to change it all. Any day we wish, we can open the book that will open our mind to new knowledge. Any day we wish, we can start a new activity. Any day we wish, we can start the process of life change. We can do it immediately, or next week, or next month, or next year.

We can also do nothing. We can pretend rather than perform. And if the idea of having to change ourselves makes us uncomfortable, we can remain as we are. We can choose rest over labour, entertainment over education, delusion over truth and doubt over confidence. The choices are ours to make. But while we curse the effect, we continue to nourish the cause. We created our circumstances by our past choices. We have both the ability and the responsibility to make better choices beginning today.

CHAPTER 6

Accepting Responsibility

As I discussed in Chapter 2, we have to create a new way of living in order to truly make this 'stuff' work. I have found there are several elements which make up this new way of living and each one is a member of my powerful mind team. Let us begin now with accepting responsibility.

The whole process of transforming your life to one of happiness and abundance begins with accepting responsibility. Accepting responsibility in your life is so important if you are to ever become empowered to create and experience a life that can be truly defined as fulfilled. By accepting responsibility, I mean you must take responsibility for *all* your results, both your successes and your failures.

As time has gone by, I have realised just how many people are not aware of the fact that they are creating the events, conditions and circumstances that are being experienced due to previously established beliefs and subconscious programming. The majority believe that many aspects of their lives are out of their personal ability to control or are left to 'chance' or 'fate'.

It is exactly these types of self-limiting and falsely established beliefs, that many have been taught throughout their lives, which keep so many people seemingly stuck in continually unfulfilling situations and circumstances. This fact, combined with a lack of awareness, is precisely why so many experience limiting outcomes.

If *you* want to create the life of your dreams, then *you* are going to have to take responsibility for your life as well. That means giving up all your excuses, all the reasons why you can't and why you haven't up until now and all your blaming of outside circumstances.

Whatever has gone on before, all that matters now is that from this point forward you choose to take responsibility and give your life positive direction.

First steps

To begin, let's look at a situation that most will recognise. In the case of alcoholism or drug addiction, all of the major institutions that treat such conditions agree that the first step in effectively overcoming these life-altering situations is the willingness of the patient to recognise and admit that a problem exists. The second step is accepting sole responsibility for the creation of the existing situation, so that it can be properly treated, dealt with and eventually overcome.

Without that initial recognition or awareness, it is impossible for the person to accept personal responsibility, as they believe that someone or some circumstance outside of their control caused them to fall into the addiction. As long as this belief remains and they deny personal responsibility, it is impossible to effectively treat the condition and it is likely that the same addiction will resurface at some other point in their life.

It is *essential* for a person to accept the fact that they are experiencing the outcome based on choices that they freely made and that they have the individual power within them to overcome the current condition. Until that awareness is realised and established as belief, nothing can be done in the long term to change the consequences that these situations create.

To effectively treat addictions, the person must accept responsibility and choose to give their life new positive direction. This is the first step in learning to create, achieve and experience a life of abundance and happiness.

Developing your awareness

By expanding your awareness in the areas covered in my book thus far, you will have already made tremendous progress in developing a much deeper and extremely self-empowering understanding of your limitless capability.

Accepting responsibility and expanding that truth, and discovering your limitless capabilities, will prove to be the most freeing and self-empowering decision you could ever make. It most certainly was for me!

When we change the way we think, when we change the way we look at things and when we change the way we behave, our results change.

In taking these concepts further, I hope the following pointers will be helpful.

Accepting personal responsibility includes:

- Acknowledging that you are solely responsible for the choices in your life

- Accepting that only you are responsible for what you choose to feel or think

- Accepting that you alone choose the direction of your life

- Accepting that you cannot blame others for the choices that you have made

- Tearing down the mask of defence or rationale that *others* are responsible for who you are, what has happened to you and what you are bound to become

- Pointing the finger of responsibility back to you and away from others

- Realising that you determine your feelings about any events or actions addressed to you, no matter how negative they seem

- Recognising that you are your best 'fan'; it is not reasonable or healthy for you to depend on others to make you feel good about yourself

- Recognising that as you enter adulthood and maturity, you determine how your self-esteem will develop

- Not feeling sorry for the 'rough deal' you have been handed but taking hold of your life and giving it direction and reason

- Letting go of your sense of over-responsibility for others

- Protecting and nurturing your health and emotional wellbeing

- Taking an honest inventory of your strengths, abilities, talents, virtues and positive points

- Developing positive, self-affirming, self-talk scripts to enhance your personal development and growth

- Letting go of blame and anger towards those in your past

- Working through anger, hostility, pessimism and depression over past hurts, pains, abuse, mistreatment and misdirection.

When you have not accepted personal responsibility, you can run the risk of becoming:

- Overly dependent on others for recognition, approval, affirmation and acceptance

- Chronically hostile, angry or depressed over how unfairly you have been or are being treated

- Fearful about ever taking a risk or making a decision

- Overwhelmed by disabling fears

- Unsuccessful at the enterprises you take on in life

- Unsuccessful in personal relationships

- Emotionally or physically unhealthy

- Addicted to the abuse of food and unhealthy substances such as alcohol and drugs

- Unable to develop trust or to feel secure with others.

What do people believe who have not accepted personal responsibility?

- It's not my fault. I am the way I am.

- I never asked to be born.

- I want you to fix me.

- Life is unfair! There is no sense in trying to take control of my life.

- Why go on; I see no use in it.

- You can't help me, nobody can help me. I'm useless and a failure.

- When do the troubles and problems cease? I'm tired of all this.

- Life is so depressing. If only I had better luck and had been born to a healthier/wealthier family or attended a better school or had a better job, etc.

- How can you say that I am responsible for what happens to me in the future? There is fate, luck, politics,

greed, envy, wicked and jealous people and other negative influences that have a greater bearing on my
future than I have.

- How can I ever be happy, seeing how bad my life has
been?

- My parents made me who I am today!

- The problems in my family have influenced who I am
and what I will be; there is nothing I can do to change
that.

- Racism, bigotry, prejudice, sexism, ageism and
closed-mindedness all stand in the way of my becoming what I really want to be.

- No matter how hard I work, I will never get ahead.

- You have to accept the luck of the draw.

**In order to accept personal responsibility,
you need to develop the ability to:**

- Seek out and to accept help for yourself

- Be open to new ideas or concepts about life and the
human condition

- Refute irrational beliefs and overcome fears

- Affirm yourself positively

- Recognise that you are the sole determinant of the choices you make

- Recognise that you choose your responses to the people, actions and events in your life

- Let go of anger, fear, blame, mistrust and insecurity

- Take risks and become open to change and growth in your life

- Take off the masks of behavioural characteristics behind which you hide your low self-esteem

- Reorganise your priorities and goals

- Realise that you are in charge of the direction your life takes.

The tools, tips and aids to these statements are to be found in the remaining chapters of my book.

CHAPTER 7

Letting Go

Letting go is another crucial member of my powerful mind team. I had learnt how holding on to past negative experiences was so destructive, but once I put into practice the various techniques I discuss in this chapter, my life was transformed.

Carrying negative experiences

We all go through positive and negative experiences during our lives. Sadly, most of us hang on to or constantly recall negative experiences, some of which go back years, perhaps even all the way back to childhood.

Other unpleasant or negative situations may have happened yesterday or six months ago. Something someone did may have angered you, caused you to build up resentment, seek revenge, etc. When we hold on to these negative experiences we actually block our ability to move forward and heal.

When you hang on to a negative or unpleasant experience, if you don't let go of it, you are naturally thinking about it and it is something that is regularly on your mind. I'm not talking about memories; we all have memories. But how many memories do you recall regularly? How many pleasant memories do you recall every day? Chances are you're like most people and you have a number of unpleasant experiences that you're holding on to, from a traumatic childhood event to a recent fight with a friend that means you no longer speak to each other.

These are the kinds of things many people carry – but the more you carry the worse life gets – it's that simple.

Anger and resentment drains your energy and keeps you imprisoned in your past. By choosing to let go of your hurt and anger you give yourself the freedom to fully experience joy in life. We've all seen the person who blows up at the smallest incident. It is the accumulation of built-up, unreleased anger that causes this explosion.

Learning how to let go by focusing on what you want

You can begin to let go by simply getting your mind to focus on something different. It's not about saying: I let go of the pain from my fight with X – and moving on. That will help, but if you really want to start moving on then you also have to get your mind to focus on new things, and in the process you automatically let go of the negative events and situations that have been slowing you down.

Start focusing on what you *want* to happen. Let go of the past and negative situations by getting your mind to focus on different things. Direct your subconscious mind to help you let go by giving it new instructions.

I had to do exactly this when I was left to bring up my three children without any financial support whatsoever. If I had allowed my thoughts to dwell on this, it would not only have made me angry but the negative emotions would also have been very destructive in what I was attracting into my life. Instead I learnt to focus my thoughts on what I could do to give my kids the life I hoped to give them and not rely on anyone else. Of course, as time went by, everything started to flow in the right direction.

I have frequently heard people grumble about how little support they get towards their children from their ex-partners. While I can appreciate where they are coming from, sadly all they do is make themselves more unhappy, negatively affecting the vibrational frequency they emit when their ex-partner is probably happily getting on with life!

Today, researchers are looking into how holding on to negative feelings and emotions impacts the nervous system and the cells of our bodies. They believe that if you hold on to negative feelings and sad emotions or depressing memories, there's a chance that you could reshape the human cell – to the point where your thoughts of the past have an adverse impact on your cells and your physical health. It seems that hanging on to negative past events can destroy your life in ways you're not even aware of.

Of course there will have been negative things that have happened and I'm not asking you to ignore them; acknowledge them because they did happen.

But ask yourself these questions:

- Does hanging on to them serve me any purpose?

- Does hanging on to them help me move forwards?

- Does hanging on to them work in my favour in any way?

If you said no to any or all of these questions then tell yourself this: 'This emotion/feeling doesn't help me, so I'm letting it go and focusing on what is more positive and important.'

This is one of the hardest things to do. We know we should do it, and we beat ourselves up inside when we don't do it, and this of course just makes the problem keep coming back. When we dwell on an issue for too long, it hurts our hearts and keeps us from being fully present in the moment. When we are not fully present in the now, we aren't living our lives to the fullest and we are not free.

You know this already, but when you're dragging yourself down with a past event that has haunted you, or still is haunting you, you often cannot see a way forward. You feel trapped. You ask yourself, 'Will this never end?' You want to be free, but you feel too hopeless to see that there really is a way out, a way to let go of an obsessive thought, or of the guilt you feel when you've blamed yourself, or the anger you feel from blaming another.

You may find yourself in a stressful situation that you fear will never end or you fear you just cannot get on with your life because of a particular situation. It may be true that a past or ongoing event really has no 'end' to it. Your life and the challenges in it will never truly be over and done with until your life is over. There are just going to be some things (and people) in life that you have no control over and sometimes you just have to accept that. But I'm now going to describe to you how you can let go of worrying, let go of the past or the ongoing event, so that you can be more present and get on with your life in a more positive, accepting and productive manner.

Getting complete

This process is called 'getting complete' with the issue. What does getting complete mean? It means that at any given moment you are a complete person, independent of your past, your situations or what others think of you. Being complete means you can let go. Letting go empowers you to be responsible for your own life and your choices about who you are and what you do. I'll tell you a way to get complete, but first you have to be willing to allow yourself to try something new. If you are willing to do this, then you've taken the first step. Below, I have outlined a very simple, yet very effective technique, similar to a guided meditation, on how to have some completion in your life so that you may let go. (Meditation is when you sit with eyes closed and empty your mind to attain inner peace and relaxation and a guided meditation is when you visualise and focus on a specific thought or situation. I'll discuss this in more detail in Chapter 11.)

Firstly, do whatever you need to do to have 15 minutes or so alone, somewhere quiet where you can relax, even if it's just in the shower. (Later when you have had more practice with this, you'll find you can do it in a matter of moments, wherever you are.) Take a couple of deep breaths to help clear your mind and focus on the issue for which you are seeking closure. If you find writing things down helps you think, then please consider writing out all your responses to the following thoughts as you go through them.

Now think to yourself, 'What is the pleasure of . . . [this issue]?' Try to think of all the good things you enjoyed from this issue that you are focusing on with this exercise. Often there isn't any pleasure in it and that's why you're doing the completion. Nevertheless, you might find you like the adrenaline rush, or that it's easier to sit in your suffering rather than face the fear of the unknown, etc. Whatever it is, notice what you feel, the sensations in your body, the emotions and know that whatever you feel (or don't feel) is OK.

Now think, 'What is NOT the pleasure of [this issue]?' Here's where most of your complaints are. Notice how you feel when you think about the issue. Are you feeling sad, anxious, angry or numb? Whatever you feel is OK. Just notice all the thoughts, images and emotions that come up. If you have a lot of intensity here, sit with it until it begins to shift and subside.

Then think about all of the people involved that you need to forgive regarding this issue. Include yourself in this, since self-forgiveness is often the hardest one. Try to allow yourself to forgive even the people who you don't think deserve it. If you can do this even a little bit, it will help you. This is something you have to feel inside of you. You can't just say 'I forgive you', with words. You may have to sit with this for a few minutes, if it is difficult and uncomfortable.

Next, think about all of the people you need to *thank* regarding this issue. This may seem impossible in some cases, but try it nevertheless. You may even have to just thank the person who gave you the motivation or perseverance to come as far as you have already. Or just be thankful for the lessons you have learned through all of this. This is a time to be grateful.

Now it is finally time to let go. Imagine your issue being sealed up inside a balloon, which floats off into the sky until you cannot see it any more. Let yourself just feel empty, with the issue gone into the universe to become recycled energy. Take some deep breaths. Finally, you need to fill that space within you, where that issue was; do not leave it empty. Fill the space with something that is pleasurable to you. You choose; some ideas would be more joy, love, compassion or peace. Open your heart to allow yourself to receive. When you feel complete for the time being, then you *are* complete.

Repeat this procedure whenever you feel the need for some completion, even if you have to do it over again for the same issue, at a later time. You'll feel more empowered to be in control of your own life, which is the only thing you can control. When you choose to be complete and are able to let go, you are choosing your own destiny and happiness and then you are truly free.

Forgiveness

Forgiveness is an incredibly powerful and self-liberating principle, which, when properly implemented, allows a sense of peace and overall wellbeing to flow and permeate your innermost being. Many people do not appreciate that when someone makes the choice to hold resentment or 'non-forgiveness' against another, they are not hurting the person that they are holding the resentment against, but instead only hurting themselves.

Normally we think of forgiveness as us forgiving others who have wronged us in some way. However, it is equally as important to develop the ability to forgive yourself for past mistakes that you have made and perceive and hold as guilt.

Let's look at how and why a state of non-forgiveness has the ability to affect your external reality and has a direct impact on what you manifest in

your life. As you have discovered in the previous
chapters, all things, both seen and unseen, broken
down into their most basic sub-atomic structures,
consist of pure energy or vibration. These vibrations,
based on the specific formation or structure of these
sub-atomic particles that make them up, resonate
and broadcast a particular frequency or rate of
vibration.

As an example, love creates and emanates a very
different vibrational frequency than hate. Forgiveness
resonates and emanates a different vibrational frequency than non-forgiveness. Regardless of the
frequency or vibratory rate that results, these vibrations or frequencies that you experience are sent out
into the universe and are attracted to energies of a
similar or equal vibratory pattern that join together
and form what you come to see and experience in
your physical world.

As we have discovered your thoughts also consist
of and broadcast a specific vibratory frequency
based on and determined by the quality of thought
and emotion. This attracts into your life the events,
conditions and circumstances that you see manifesting in your physical world every minute of every
day.

By failing to forgive yourself or someone else who
may have wronged you in some way, you are actually creating a vibratory frequency through those

thoughts of non-forgiveness and resentment, which are being broadcast, attracting similar vibratory patterns or frequencies, in this case resentment and non-forgiveness.

To take it a step further, if you are not only holding on to resentment or non-forgiveness towards another, but also 'hoping or wishing' that some negative experience be inflicted on them, you are in reality asking and will receive the outcome of that desire in your own life in some form. How is that possible? Because the energy that you are creating is being internalised in you and as a result you will attract additional energies that support those thoughts.

Through purposefully and consciously implementing forgiveness into your life and beginning to exercise an attitude of gratitude for whatever experiences you may encounter, you will begin to realise and personally experience your ability to consciously attract and create your life by *design* rather than by *default*.

Unconditional love and forgiveness is the essence of our Source, our 'being' or whatever you may perceive that to be dependent upon your religious beliefs, for example God, Buddha, etc. By developing the ability to forgive unconditionally, you will have made tremendous and powerful progress in your ability to begin experiencing a life of ease, harmony and overall wellbeing.

What forgiveness does NOT mean

It is important to consider what forgiveness does NOT mean. Forgiveness does not mean you allow people to treat you badly. It does not mean you ignore the wrongdoings. It does mean you accept that the person has made a mistake and you are choosing to grant them mercy. When you forgive someone, you won't necessarily forget the hurt. In addition, forgiveness does not mean you are condoning or excusing the person's behaviour and doesn't mean that you have to trust that person again. Some acts, like physical and sexual abuse, require that you limit your trust or at least test the trust with the person who hurt you. Remember, forgiveness is more for you than the other person.

Releasing anger

Let's have a look at another process that will help you let go and forgive. This is the process of releasing anger.

First, you must face and release the anger that you feel. On the surface of the hurt is anger and you must break away that layer first. Underneath the anger is the pain and hurt that you must grieve. There are many ways to release anger and hurt. You can talk about it with trusted people. You can pray about it and ask God to take away that pain and resentment. You can express your feelings to the person who hurt you, provided that it's possible to have a healthy conversation where both you and the other person speak and listen to each other in respectful ways.

One of the best and most cleansing ways to release your negative feelings is to write a letter to your perpetrator. In this letter, you pour out every emotion you feel. You tell them everything that hurt you and everything they did to make you angry. Do not hold anything back. Allow yourself to really feel the anger and cry the tears by reading it out loud to yourself. When you are done, burn or bury the letter as a symbol that you are ready to move on. DO NOT give the letter to the person. This letter is for you and only you.

After processing all your emotions, you are ready to make the choice to forgive. It is a choice that requires compassion, understanding and an open and loving heart. Each of us makes mistakes in life. At one time or another (probably more than one time), we will hurt another person. Maybe it will be unintentional, or perhaps it will be a purposeful reaction to someone hurting you. When this does happen, do you want to be forgiven? Do you want another chance to make amends? Most people don't mean to hurt us – they are dealing with their own pain and unresolved resentment. It's unfortunate that often we take it out on our loved ones, but until we break the cycle it will continue to happen.

Cutting the cords

Another highly effective process you may like to try comes from a book written by a friend of mine, Anne Jones. Anne is an international healer and author of several books. The following is extracted from her book *Opening Your Heart* and is called 'cutting the cords'.

In this visualisation, you will dissolve the cords and hooks that are binding you and forgive.

Find a quiet place where you won't be disturbed and make yourself comfortable. You may like to get a friend to read the words that follow and take you through this stage of the process.

- Breathe in deeply four times – deep into your solar plexus. Drop your shoulders and relax.

- See yourself walking up to the gate of a walled garden – this is your personal healing garden. Open the gate and step inside. Your garden is filled with flowers and lawns; it is serene, tranquil and totally private.

- Start to follow a path as it leads you deeper into your garden. You go deeper and deeper until you come to a walled courtyard. There is a fountain playing in the centre and roses grow on the walls. There is peace in this inner sanctum. You see a bench and sit down; relax.

- Call in now the person or people you wish to release and see them enter the far side of the courtyard.

- Between you and each one is a cord [might be good to describe it]. You pick up the scissors that are on the bench beside you. Cut through the cord. The connection is now broken.

- See a stream of dark energy now leaving your heart centre; it flows like a river, taking any residual negative feelings away from you. See it flowing into sunlight and gradually turning into light. Keep the stream flowing until it is leaving you as light. Your bitterness has now turned to light and wisdom.

- Move towards the person and tell them that you forgive them and are setting yourself and them free. All energetic and emotional connections are now released and you are free.

- Place your hand over your heart centre and imagine a stream of healing energies flowing from your hand into your heart to ease the pain there.

- Gradually you will feel the hurting in your heart subside. Now you can leave the garden in your own time, slowly and gently. Welcome back into the room.

A real-life example

An incredibly profound example of hanging on to resentment and not being able to let go and forgive comes from work done by American author Byron Katie, and related in her book *Loving What Is*. She was helping a woman who was the victim of a horrific gang rape 20 years ago. All these years later, she is still hanging on to that resentment and has barely moved forward in her life.

> Byron asked her, 'How long did that rape last?'
> She replied, 'Maybe 30 minutes.'
> 'And how long have you been holding on to it?'
> 'About 20 years.'
> 'So who's been raping you longer? Them or you?'

What a powerful question from Byron Katie to this woman!

Don't continue blocking yourself from all of the abundance in life by holding on to your resentment.

Emotional freedom technique

Diane Egby-Edwards (see Chapter 5) introduced me to a process called emotional freedom technique (EFT) after I went to see her one day several years ago because I was very hurt and angry about someone's behaviour towards me. Diane took me through the EFT process and I could not believe the results. I left feeling calm and peaceful!

There are many EFT practitioners out there, but it is a technique you can do yourself and it can be highly effective. There are many books and lots of information on the subject available on the internet. In order to explain this clearly, I have taken the following explanation of EFT from a holistic studies report by Drs Phillip and Jane Mountrose of the Awakenings Institute (www.gettingthru.org).

Understanding how emotional healing with EFT works may require an open mind for many people. The effectiveness of EFT only makes sense if it is related to the human energy system. Fortunately, you don't have to believe any of this to receive the positive benefits of using these techniques.

In addition to having a physical body that is fuelled by food, we humans also run on an intricate energy system, which is fuelled by electrical impulses that run through the body. This energy system holds the key to many of the disturbances that we experience in our daily lives. When this energy system is out of balance, our emotional life could be compared to a car that is in desperate need of a tune-up. The result may take the form of any type of emotional disturbance including phobias, anger, depression, grief, guilt, anxiety and a full range of fears, to name a few examples. There may also be physical symptoms such as pain, headaches, asthma and tension that are related to these emotions.

EFT provides relief from the majority of these disturbances, often in minutes, and the results are usually long-lasting. In fact, it frequently provides relief where other techniques fail and has a high success rate, typically 80 per cent or better.

EFT is based on a revolutionary new discovery that violates most of the beliefs of conventional psychology and contends that the cause of all negative emotions is a disruption in the body's energy system. EFT relieves symptoms by an unusual (but scientific) routine of tapping with the fingertips on a short series of points on the body that correspond to acupuncture points on the energy meridians. Where there is an imbalance, there is a corresponding blockage in the flow of energy through the meridian system.

The tapping serves to release the blockages that are created when a person thinks about or becomes involved in an emotionally disturbing circumstance. When this blockage is released, the emotions come again into balance. Once balanced, the person cannot get upset about the circumstance, no matter how hard they try. The memory remains but the charge is gone. Typically, the result is long-lasting and the person's awareness usually changes in a positive way as a natural result of the healing.

Most energetic imbalances may be partially or completely relieved within a short time using this process. Others may be relieved through repetition of the process.

How to release a problem using EFT

The emotional freedom technique as practised by Diane is split into two parts:

- Identifying the problem
- Releasing the problem

In order to identify the problem Diane sat me down and asked me to start thinking about and visualising the situation that had made me so angry and upset. I spent a couple of minutes focusing on it until my emotion got to its strongest. You can do the same with a situation that is concerning you, whether it is a feeling of hurt, anger, jealousy, fear, etc., you should focus on it and build that emotion within you.

When you feel the emotion at its strongest say out loud the following statement: 'Even though I [state your problem here, e.g. feel hatred towards my parents/partner, have a phobia of spiders, dread public speaking, drink too much, etc.], I truly, deeply and absolutely forgive, accept and love myself.'

Using two or three fingers of one of your hands, gently tap on the points shown on the diagram on page 128 while saying out loud the above statement as you tap on each of the points.

Next, in releasing the problem, you insert the phrase that describes your problem into the following statement, saying it out loud as before and going through the tapping process on the above points again. 'Even though I have this [insert problem, emotion, belief], I now choose to let it go and remain [insert as necessary].'

Here is an example, 'Even though I have this feeling of hurt and anger, I now choose to let it go and remain calm and comfortable.'

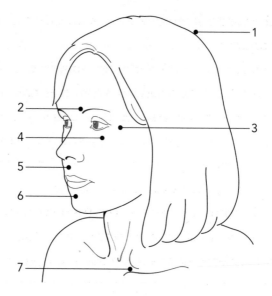

1. The top–back part of your scalp/your crown.
2. The inner side of your eyebrow.
3. The outer side of your eye.
4. Below your eye socket/on your cheekbone.
5. The middle of your 'moustache' area.
6. In between your chin and your lower lip.
7. The inner tip of your collarbone.
8. Under your armpit.
9. The 'karate chop' side of your palm.

Tips for tapping

Tap as gently as possible but do not merely 'touch' those points. If you find that it hurts to tap, then you should decrease the 'impact' of your tapping.

To tap, use whatever number of fingers that is comfortable for you – either by using only your index finger, your index and middle fingers or your index, middle and ring fingers altogether.

You don't have to get the exact tapping spot 100 per cent correct. Usually tapping around the prescribed tapping points will achieve the same results. Intuitively you will find which the best tapping spots are for you as you practise the process. Continue tapping on each point for as long as it takes you to say the words.

You will find that the more you do this process, the better it gets – and you will feel even better in your later sessions than your earlier sessions, as it is a cumulative process.

Now of course this is not meant as an authoritative guide to EFT as there are many EFT therapists and each one has a slightly different way of doing it. However, the above process certainly works well for me and has played a major part over the years in helping me move forwards.

Hypnotherapy in simple terms

Diane Egby-Edwards has also achieved amazing results through her work as a hypnotherapist. I asked her to explain how it works and she told me that most of the time we are able to account and give good reasons for many of the problems that we experience. For instance, a person who suffers low self-esteem may give as the cause the awful occasion at school when they were thoroughly humiliated in class by the teacher in front of all the other children.

However, some issues may be buried deep in the subconscious mind, she explained, so deeply buried that we have no 'conscious' awareness of the original problem, but nevertheless we are manifesting the emotional responses to those issues in our everyday lives. Sometimes it is less painful to 'forget' a trauma than to 'remember' it.

Sadly, these 'forgotten' memories are still with us and can be responsible for us having inappropriate feelings or out-of-proportion responses to situations in life. Examples include having an over-the-top response to a comment that someone makes, holding strong prejudices, being anxious and afraid for no apparent reason, fearing rejection, nightmares, nail biting, etc. – the list is endless. If you are unable to recall a memory that explains the cause of your emotional response, it usually means that inside you there is a subconscious issue that has never been properly resolved.

Diane went on to explain that hypnosis is an altered state of consciousness that works on a *subconscious* level. She told me that there is nothing to fear and much to be gained so long as you work with a skilled hypnotherapist, 'In good hypnosis we are able to review those traumas, and often we find that the original memory is not as bad as we feared. That's because we are looking at it now with adult eyes, but to the four-year-old child, for example, it was much more upsetting.'

Hypnosis in itself feels great and most people start to experience good changes straight away. In hypnosis your conscious, thinking mind is still active, you don't 'zonk off to the planet Zod', yet your subconscious mind is much more available to you. That's why hypnotherapy works very quickly – problems can be resolved more speedily with hypnosis than with any other treatment. Usually just a few sessions can bring about the necessary healing.

Diane's passion for her work shines through as she explained, 'After treatment with a good hypnotherapist you will feel a wonderful sense of release – you will feel different – the world will feel like a different place and you will wish you'd done it sooner. Life is a precious gift, far too precious to be weighed down with sorrow and fear or any of the other negative feelings from the past.'

Live in the present

Truly, the only place to live is in the present, and to live joyously is our natural state of being. Anything less than this state is a negative condition of pain that needs to be healed.

This is the final step to 'letting go' – to live in the present moment – that is, to start living in the now.

You may have heard of this before but note that living 'in the now' is different to living 'for the moment'. Living in the now is the process of enjoying everything that is going on at this present moment. It means creating your future in the present moment – while still enjoying everything that is happening.

Take a look around you and appreciate those things that you once thought were trivial. Take some extra time to enjoy a few moments of the day doing something completely different but really putting all of yourself into it.

When you are here, now, you can be nowhere else. You are not hanging on to something – you are not holding on to a past event. You are here now. I know some of you may say something like the following, 'I hate where I am now; I don't want to think about it.'

Where you are now is unpleasant because you are looking at all the negative things going on. Focus on a few of the positive things, which can be anything from nature to the wonderful family you may have. This forces your mind to look at things differently and tells your subconscious mind that you are ready for new possibilities. You will begin emanating a more positive vibrational frequency.

Letting go of the past and learning to live in the present moment, in the now, was a great break-through for me and once I 'got there', suddenly and unexpectedly, life became very easy and extremely enjoyable.

CHAPTER 8

The Power of Visualisation

Another key member of my powerful mind team is visualisation. Once I understood the power of visualisation, I became very aware of what I was picturing in my mind and how to make it work for me, not against me!

What is visualisation?

Visualisation is the single most powerful capability that the human being has. By visualisation I mean the act of creating vivid pictures in your mind. We all do it, all of the time.

Visualisation, just like natural law (see Chapter 3), works for everyone. What is important to remember at this point is that whether or not you are consciously aware of it, you are continuously visualising and creating what you see in your physical world, either through your conscious or subconscious thoughts. Most people just aren't aware of what they are creating. They are unconsciously creating the daily events, conditions and circumstances that they come to experience in their lives and aren't even aware they are doing it. I also believe in the power of visualisation for healing and wellbeing (see Chapter 11).

Your thoughts are causing you to visualise in words, pictures or feelings, either consciously or unconsciously, the events and circumstances that you see and experience in your life on a daily basis. So you may as well start to become aware and consciously visualise and begin to create the things you desire, rather than leaving it to chance or unconsciously creating what you do not want in your life.

Planting and nurturing the seed

Absolutely nothing in our world can grow without a seed first being planted. It is against any and all scientific or spiritual law.

As we have already seen, your thoughts represent the seed, which, through repetition, establishes the beliefs that you hold. The combination of those thoughts and beliefs are the ingredients that determine your emotions. Your visualisation, goal setting (more on this in Chapter 9) and positive affirmations (more on this in Chapter 10) represent the nurturing of that seed. Depending on the specific seeds that you are planting, how you nurture the seeds that you plant determines what you will come to see and experience in your physical world, regardless of whether you are doing it consciously or unconsciously.

Visualisation is probably the most under-utilised personal tool that you possess. If you make use of it, it will greatly accelerate the achievement of any success in several powerful ways:

- It activates your subconscious mind, which will start to generate creative ideas to achieve your goals.

- It activates the law of attraction, thereby drawing into your life the people, resources and circumstances you will need to succeed.

- It builds your internal motivation to take the necessary actions to manifest your dreams.

- It programmes your brain to more readily perceive and recognise the resources you will need.

Why does it work?

So, why does visualisation work? What is it about learning to visualise that makes it so important and valuable? The answer is quite simple: it's a matter of how the mind works and translates information.

When you look at something, the centre of your brain, the visual cortex, fires. It takes the different spectra of light that you are looking at and translates them into a picture that you are able to understand. Here's the interesting part though. When you take the time to visualise something, your mind uses the exact same visual cortex to see those pictures in your mind's eye. To your brain, there is no difference between what your eyes are seeing out there and what your mind is seeing in here. Your mind and your body take both of those pictures and label them as the same thing.

This is very useful because you can begin to use your visualisation to convince your mind and body that everything you want is already a part of your life. This begins to put your body and mind into alignment with having that thing you desire.

So, if your mind is unable to tell the difference between a daydream in your head and a book that sits on your desk and is viewed by your eyes, then you can begin to use your visualisation to attract the things you want. As you begin to do this, your body and emotions begin to vibrate at a level that allows you to feel the feelings of having what it is you want. This vibration goes out into the universe and the universe begins to line things up in order for that visualisation to become a reality. The universe *must* respond to that vibration and it will. It will begin to deliver things that will allow you to maintain that vibration. Isn't the mind an amazing thing?

Visualisation in practice

Even though none of us were taught this at school, sports psychologists and peak performance experts have been promoting the power of visualisation since the 1980s. Almost all Olympic and professional athletes now incorporate the power of visualisation in their training.

British athlete Sally Gunnell OBE, winner of an Olympic gold medal, has said that she visualised herself winning in her mind over one hundred times before she even set foot on the track.

People who are successful in business use the power of visualisation all the time, but many are unaware just how much this powerful technique is really helping them.

Cosmic ordering

So, what is the most effective way to do this? Different teachers have different opinions about this. For example, some people say, 'Just want it. Let it go. Then go out and have a good time.' You may well have heard about cosmic ordering. There are several books written on the subject. These suggest that you literally 'demand' of the universe that which you require and then trust and expect that it will arrive.

A great analogy of this is when you are in a restaurant: you place your order with the waiter and you sit and wait for your meal to arrive. You totally trust and expect that what you have ordered will be brought to your table. You don't for a moment expect a completely different meal to arrive, do you?

Daily disciplines

The cosmic ordering technique works for many, but that is not my way of doing things. I've always had what I call these 'daily disciplines', which include waking up in the morning and visualising my goals as already complete. I believe in sending a constant message.

I learnt from Jack Canfield, author of *Chicken*

Soup for the Soul and *The Success Principles*, that the daily discipline of visualisation does a number of things. First, it reprogrammes your subconscious mind and, second, it programmes the reticular activating system in your brain to start letting into your awareness anything that will help you achieve your goals.

The reticular activating system is just a big fancy name for a group of cells in your brain that pick up all the sensory input from your external world and filter things out of or into your field of perception.

If you think of Google Search engine, when you type in a word in Google, it searches the internet for everything that relates to that word and brings it back to you in seconds. The reticular activating system works 800 times faster than your conscious cells do. It works faster than the speed of light and it picks up all the vibrations, all the sensory input from your environment and, if it is important to you, it sends a signal to your consciousness to alert you. For example, mothers can sleep through a lot of traffic noise outside their house, but their baby makes one peep and they wake up. This is because their reticular activating system is programmed to let the sound of their baby through that filter, but not the sound of the traffic outside because that's not important to them.

So when you start to programme into the reticular activating system what it is that you want and you focus on it, you're instructing your brain to find it and alert you to it.

The problem is that the reticular system is programmed to let in things that match your self-image. So if you have a negative self-image, you're not going to let in opportunities that could make you a millionaire, for example, because you can't even perceive those. They don't get through.

The reticular activating system is a powerful tool, but it can only look for ways to achieve the exact pictures you give it. Your creative subconscious doesn't think in words – it can only think in pictures. So how does this help your effort to become successful and achieve the life of your dreams?

When you give your brain specific, colourful and vividly compelling pictures to manifest it will seek out and capture all of the information necessary to bring that picture into reality for you. If you give it pictures of a beautiful home, a loving partner, an exciting career and wonderful holidays, it will go to work on achieving those.

By contrast, if you are constantly feeding it negative, fearful and anxious pictures, guess what? It will achieve those, too. This is called worrying. What happens to our bodies when we worry? We tense up, disrupt our normal breathing and psycho-physically prepare ourselves for failure. Instead, learn to use positive visualisation to prepare yourself for success. As you do, you will transform the energy that supports your worrying into fuel for making your dreams come true.

Of course, one common question people ask is, 'If I am not wealthy and successful, how can I lie to myself and imagine that I am wealthy and successful?' And that's a very fair question. When I was desperately unhappy and frightened for my future, I initially also found it very hard to imagine myself living a happy and abundant life, when in reality it was the complete opposite!

So let's now look at some useful tips on how you can get visualisation to work for you rather than against you.

Practice and discipline

Repetition is the key to success in acquiring any new skills. You have to practise your visualisation skills. The good news is, the more real your visualisation, the more effectively you will achieve what you desire. Remember, you will only ever achieve as far as your thoughts and your imagination take you, so practise and work on yourself. It's worth it.

Also, remember how in Chapter 2 we learnt about alpha brain waves? The most effective visualisation takes place when your brain is emitting alpha waves, which naturally occur when one is in a state of relaxation.

The end result

Always visualise yourself as if you have already achieved your dream and don't 'see' it in the future.

Visualise yourself as the new slim you, in your new car (exact model and colour), with the new job, in your wonderful home, etc. Always visualise the end result even when you are probably unaware in the beginning how you are going to get there. The key is to trust that the universe and life will unfold and the route will become clear.

In *Chicken Soup for the Soul*, Jack Canfield draws on a very helpful analogy of a journey. For example, you may be in Bournemouth (in the south of the UK) and you want to get to Aberdeen (in the north). You are setting off in a car at night; it is pitch black and your headlights only light up the road 100 to 200 metres ahead of you. You trust that you will get to Aberdeen, because that is where you want to get to. However, all you have to see is the next 200 metres ahead of you. That is exactly how life tends to unfold before us. If you just trust that the next 200 metres will unfold after that and so on, your life will keep unfolding, and it will eventually get you to the destination of whatever it is you truly want.

Metaphors

Some people like to use metaphors in their visualisations.

A man I know was very unhappy at work and he told me that he visualised himself digging through a tunnel; that he could see the light at the end of the tunnel, but never seemed to get any closer to it. I quickly told him to change that vision. I said, 'I want you to see yourself *out* of the tunnel, in the daylight, celebrating the success of having made it.' He quickly realised where he had been going wrong. Within a couple of months, his work situation had turned around and he was so much happier.

Put emotions into your dream

Whatever your dream, always *feel* what you are visualising. Of course, the emotions you attach to your visualisation must be a positive vibration.

Visualise and feel the image of the world you want to live in, and this multiplies the effect many times over.

You can also add sounds, smells and tastes to your pictures to make them more vivid.

Remember to visualise how great you are going to feel as if you have already achieved your dream. Then you will be emanating the right vibrational frequency to attract that which you desire into your life.

These emotions are what propel your vision forwards. Researchers know that when accompanied by intense emotions, an image or scene can stay locked in the memory for ever. The more passion, excitement and energy you can muster, the more powerful the ultimate result will be.

See yourself as a third person

Imagine you are watching a movie in your mind. You are the lead actor or actress in this movie. You are viewing your life as a third person.

Go through the following three steps:

Imagine sitting in the theatre or cinema; the lights dim and then the movie starts. It is a film of you, doing perfectly whatever it is that you want to do better. See as much detail as you can create, including your clothing, the expression on your face, small body movements, the environment and any other people that might be around. Add in any sounds you would be hearing – traffic, music, other people talking, cheering. Finally, recreate in your body any feelings you think you would be experiencing as you engage in this activity.

Get out of your chair, walk up to the screen, open a door in the screen and enter into the movie. Now experience the whole thing again from inside of yourself, looking out through your eyes. This is called an 'embodied image' rather than a 'distant image'. It will deepen the impact of the experience. Again, see everything in vivid detail, hear the sounds you would hear and feel the feelings you would feel.

Finally, walk back out of the screen that is still showing the picture of you performing perfectly, return to your seat, reach out and grab the screen and shrink it down to the size of a biscuit. Then, bring this miniature screen up to your mouth, chew it up and swallow it. Imagine that each tiny piece – just like a hologram – contains the full picture of you performing well. Imagine all these little screens travelling down into your stomach and out through the bloodstream into every cell of your body. Then imagine that every cell of your body is lit up with the movie of you performing perfectly.

When you have finished this process – it should take less than five minutes – you can open your eyes and get on with your day. If you make this part of your daily routine, you will be amazed at how much improvement you will see in your life.

Here are some further hints for your own personal movie:

Increase the colour and brightness of a wanted scene: if you increase the colour and brightness when you visualise you will increase the intensity, but make sure you only do this for something that you want and have a positive emotion about.

De-sensitise an unwanted scene: if a bad scene pops up in your movie, change it to black and white. This will help to decrease the negative emotions you feel towards the scene. Make all the images and/or people smaller and fade them away slowly.

If you don't think the movie technique is for you, don't worry. Any time spent building positive images in your mind is effective and, of course, so is diminishing the negative ones.

New habit patterns

You can also use visualisation to develop new habit patterns of self-confidence. For example, if you want to develop leadership qualities, or the ability to make decisions or have greater self-confidence, you must see yourself as if you already have those qualities and characteristics. If you find that difficult then take someone you know who already has those qualities and see yourself acting that way.

Once you begin to do that, you begin to change your self-image by replacing the picture you have in your mind of your negative habit patterns to one with this newfound positive habit pattern.

To use a common example, most people have a fear of public speaking. When I realised that I was going to be doing a lot of public speaking, I worked on myself. I visualised myself standing in front of thousands, really enjoying myself and feeling great that my speech had gone so well. My visualisation worked a treat – I now love public speaking! Apart from a burst of adrenaline before I start, I never suffer from nerves beforehand.

So, if you have an important sales meeting to go to, spend time beforehand visualising the meeting going incredibly well. Also, visualise your feeling of self-confidence and the great feeling of success when you shake hands as the deal is done.

To take another example, if you want to be more patient and loving to help your relationship, visualise yourself as being just that and seeing in your imagination the benefits of you being that kind, loving person and the change in reaction from your loved ones.

By the way, if you are concerned that you can't visualise – don't worry! There may be some people who are what psychologists describe as 'eidetic visualisers'. When they close their eyes, they see everything in bright, clear, 3D, technicolour images. Most of us, however, are non-eidetic visualisers. That means we don't really see an image as much as we just think it. That is perfectly OK. It still works just as well if you are simply *thinking* it rather than actually *seeing* it.

Creating a vision board

A vision board can help enormously with visualisation. Other common names for such tools include a dream board or perhaps a manifestation poster. Whatever the name given, it is a tool to help you manifest your desires. I have a vision board and I know of many people who also have one.

Here is some practical advice on how you can make a vision board.

The easiest way to start is by writing down a list of what it is that you want. If you don't know what you do want, then make a list of what you don't want. By knowing what you don't want, you can easily see the polar opposite and turn it into a desire. Below are some examples:

'I don't want lots of bills'	*becomes*	'I desire endless streams of money'
'I don't want to be without a relationship'	*becomes*	'I desire a fun, loving partner'

'I don't want my old car any more'	*becomes*	'I desire a brand new BMW [or whatever car you desire]'

The next stage is either to browse through relevant magazines or to go on the internet and do an image search using keywords that relate to your desire. Carefully choose some images that appeal to you and make sure they are images that really give you great feelings when you look at them.

Once you have your images, print them off, cut them out and stick them on to your vision board:

- You could use a large white poster.

- Have a pinboard on to which you pin all of your images.

- You could even stick them directly on to your wall or on the fridge door.

Where you site your vision board is quite important. You want your vision board to be close to you and in visual range as much as possible. For example, if you work from home and spend nine hours per day in your office then your office is the ideal place to put your vision board. Put it somewhere where you will often look at it.

Now you have your vision board, how often should you look at it?

I spend 15 minutes in the morning and 15 minutes in the evening looking at and visualising the desires on my vision board. This makes me feel great and often I am actually closing my eyes and taking the vision further than just staring at an image. I use the images to start my vision off and then I expand them to the depths of my desire.

Remember, the purpose of this is to feel good, so if you look at an image and it doesn't feel good then replace it with one that does. It is a trial and error process but when done repetitively, it can be very powerful. Your vision board should be an ongoing process for you and will never be complete as new desires will continue to emerge.

You should use your vision board as a 'memory jogger' to remind you to visualise and also to help you recall feelings. It is not intended to be the ultimate tool that you must use to manifest. Indeed, many deliberate creators choose not to use vision boards to help them in their visualisations and are just as successful. If it feels right for you, go ahead and enjoy creating one, but if it does not appeal to you, don't feel you need to have one.

The key point of making a vision board is to help you create powerful emotions within you. It is those emotions and feelings that are doing the manifesting, not the picture on your vision board.

Achieve your dreams

The different visualisation techniques described in this chapter can literally be used to achieve any of your dreams and goals. You can visualise your way to success in all that you do. Take lots of small steps and this will get the cycle of confidence moving in the right direction.

CHAPTER 9

The Importance of Goal Setting

Setting goals and targets in business is accepted as an important key component for success. However, I believe it crucially important to set goals in your personal life too and include this as another member of my powerful mind team.

Know your destination

Going through life without any goals is like getting into a car and driving without any destination in mind.

Would you get into your car and just start

driving, hoping to get somewhere but really not sure where you are going or how you're going to get there? How often have you got into your car and said, 'Let's just drive and see where we end up?' Chances are you're like most people – you get into your car when you need to go somewhere. Most often you know exactly where you're going and have a pretty good idea of how you're going to get there.

So why not use the same skills in life?

Life in many ways is like driving – you need to have a destination in mind. You can't get somewhere if you don't know where you're going because you'll only end up going nowhere and then wonder how you got there in the first place!

Think about that for a moment. I've seen and spoken to so many people who have lived their life without setting any goals, only to realise that where they are is not where they want to be and they have no idea how they really got there.

The frustration continues because they fail to decide where they want to go next and then never regain the enthusiasm they had for life when they were a child.

As time management author Alan Lakein has written, 'By failing to plan, they are planning to fail!'

What do you want to do?

When you were a child did you want to be a pilot, a lawyer, a vet, a pop star, a supermodel? You had such childish enthusiasm because you had a goal and you thought anything was possible. Today, you may have lost that childish enthusiasm because you no longer think that anything is possible. The only reason you lost the enthusiasm is because you didn't set goals and achieve them. Maybe you did – and maybe they were too lofty or something stopped you – but as soon as you gave up on them, you lost that enthusiasm. I'm not saying go out and try to be that pop star at 45 (although it has happened; it's not unheard of), but you can set new goals and this time do what you can to achieve them.

Often when I ask people what their goals are I get the following response: 'I don't have any goals because I don't know what I want to do.' My answer is really simple: 'You do know what you want to do – you just haven't thought about it yet.' How often do you really think about what you want to do or what you want to achieve next?

The first step is to start thinking about what you want to do or what you would like to achieve next. Now often the response to that is: 'But I don't know what I want to do next.' OK – that's fine. If you don't know exactly what you want to do or what you want to do next – then start thinking about the kind of life you want to have.

Try to look forward five years – where do you see yourself? What kind of life would you like five years from now?

Write it down. Next, start thinking about what you need to do in order to get to where you want to be in five years. You just saw what kind of life you wanted in five years – now what can you do to get there?

Now perhaps you're saying, 'I don't know what to do to get there.' My answer is, 'You do know how to get there, you just haven't thought of it yet.' My point is that once you start thinking about these kinds of things you'll begin to get answers and find solutions. You'll begin to establish a long-term goal, the life you want in five years, and you'll also set a series of short-term goals, the things you need to do to get you there. Once you do that you then have a destination in mind and an idea of how you're going to get there. The plan is to get your mind working for you rather than against you.

The reason that it's important to set goals is because without them you feel like you're just spinning your wheels in life. Without goals you no longer feel challenged, you no longer feel like you're striving for something, you no longer feel alive. Without goals life can become boring and you can lose interest, and you could end up being bored and depressed. When you have a goal or a series of goals, you suddenly feel like you have a sense of purpose. You feel like you're using your full potential and that you're striving for something better, and this helps enormously with self-confidence and self-esteem.

I'm not saying that everyone has to have lofty goals. All I'm saying is that in order to feel like you're getting the most out of life, you need to have some goals and some direction, because without them life can become meaningless.

What is your 'purpose' in life?

While goal setting is important, people often ask me how they can discover their 'purpose' in life. One of the key components to living a happy, fulfilling and rewarding life is to live your life with purpose. If you are not living a life with any purpose, you're not getting the most out of it.

When you're living a life with purpose, you have a mission. You have a reason for living.

When you have a purpose in life you will enjoy your life a great deal, but more importantly, you give your conscious mind, your subconscious mind and your spirit a mission and a direction. When your mind and spirit have this reason and direction they attract and lead you to more opportunities that will help you fulfil your purpose and enjoy life even more.

Here's how it works. When you have a purpose, you live life with a positive feeling and energy. Your subconscious mind and the universal laws pick up on this feeling, energy and purpose and begin attracting more situations, people and events that will help you fulfil that purpose so that you enjoy your life.

If you feel that every day is the same old thing, you don't get excited or you feel that you're really not living life with any sense of purpose, don't worry, you *can* turn things around.

Look at things differently

What do I mean when I say that you *can* turn things around? You can change the way that you see things.

There is a purpose to every day and each new day has some meaning in your life; you're probably just not seeing it. For example, suppose you work as a checkout cashier and you go to work every day thinking that your job has no purpose. Ultimately you feel that your life has no purpose and you're just going through the motions.

Now try looking at things in a different way. Your job as a checkout cashier helps customers make their payment quickly and easily. It helps your bosses keep track of what they sell, so that they can run their business properly. Your job also helps the company make sure that people do pay for what they want quickly and easily. You can also help make the shopping experience for the customer far more enjoyable.

Do you see how what you thought was a mundane job really has a lot of purpose – at least for that day – but only when you look at things a little differently?

Now, I know some of you may say, 'That's great – but I feel like my life overall has no purpose. Yes, I can find some purpose in my job every day – but I just don't feel like I'm living with any real purpose.'

There is a lot that you can do to help yourself live with purpose.

Time for yourself

First take a look at how you spend your day. Take a notepad and pen and write out exactly how you spend it. You can go hour by hour if you want. Then take a look and see how many hours have been set aside for *you*. This is where you get to have some time to yourself, where you can do whatever you want without anyone bothering you.

If you find you have little or no time, then you've just discovered one of the reasons why you feel you are not living life with purpose.

Too often I hear from people who say they feel they don't have any purpose, only to discover that they don't set aside any time for themselves. I'm not saying that your purpose is to do whatever you want, whenever you want, but by having some time set aside for yourself, you give yourself a chance to discover your purpose.

You also give your subconscious mind a chance to help you discover your purpose.

If you fill your day up to the point where you have no time for yourself, then you don't give yourself the opportunity to discover your purpose.

So set some time aside for yourself. Some people say, 'I come home at the end of a long day; I have three kids to feed and a husband/wife to care for. By the time I'm done I barely have energy or time for anything else.'

Fair enough, but you must try to find even five minutes for yourself. Read a book, a magazine, have a glass of something you enjoy, go for a short walk. After a week you can stretch the time to ten minutes. It's your time; just do something you want to do.

I'm not saying that this is your purpose, but when you calm down, when you are at peace, when your mind and body are at rest, in alpha state, your subconscious mind goes to work because it is no longer being bombarded with all kinds of stimuli and information that it really doesn't need.

Instead, it will help you find ways to enjoy your life and have a purpose.

'Change your glasses'

Next, try looking at your life a little differently; this is the process that some call 'changing your glasses'.

If you put on glasses that are too weak or too strong you won't see so clearly. If you wear sunglasses that are too dark or too light – how you see things will also be different. In the case of the person who has had a long day and has three kids to feed and a partner and a home to take care of, well there's already tremendous purpose here.

It may not be the ideal life that you want but there is purpose and when you recognise the purpose, you attract more positive things into your life.

Yes, you may have kids to feed or someone to care for and yes that may be the purpose for now, but if you still feel empty then you have to take some time to do what you enjoy. This won't necessarily be your purpose but by doing what you enjoy even for a few minutes a day, you'll discover or be guided to your purpose.

There is a process at work and part of that process requires that you enjoy life, relax and understand that what you focus on, you will attract.

Change the way that you see things. Start to focus on the positive aspects of your life and you'll attract more positive situations and people. Every positive thing that you do has a purpose; it has an impact on you and the people around you.

You won't see changes overnight, although I know many would like to see instant improvements. You have to get your mind and subconscious mind to work and attract the situations you need to help you improve your life. If you do this for a few weeks or months and then stop you'll end up back where you are. You have to keep on doing this until it becomes a habit, a way of life.

Goal-setting techniques

Let's have a look now at some effective goal-setting techniques. All the members of the powerful mind team, including goal setting, have to work together in the same direction in order to create the life that we want for ourselves.

State each goal as a positive statement

Express your goals in a positive way. That is a key component. How often have you been excited to accomplish a goal that didn't even sound good when you brought it up? If you are not comfortable or happy with the goals that you have set, the likelihood of you succeeding is low.

Be precise

Set a precise goal that includes starting dates, times and amounts so that you can accurately measure your achievement. If you do this, you will know exactly when you have achieved the goal and can take complete satisfaction from having achieved it.

Set priorities

When you have several goals, give each a specific priority. This helps you to avoid feeling overwhelmed by too many goals, and helps to direct your attention to the most important ones and to follow each in succession. By doing the most important first and moving through to the least important, you are enabling each task to be easier than the last. This means that the accomplishment of each task gets easier and easier, your self-confidence will grow, and this will encourage you to complete your goal.

Write goals down in the present tense, as if you have already achieved them

If you write your goals down in the present tense, this crystallises them and gives them more force. This is one of the most effective ways to get the subconscious mind to work for you.

For a daily routine, I suggest taking three to five goals and as you write each one down (remembering to do this in the present tense as if you have already achieved it), sit there for a few minutes and visualise yourself successfully achieving that goal, and really concentrate on *feeling* the emotion of success and happiness as if you have already achieved it. Here are some examples:

- I am in a wonderful loving relationship with a man who [be as specific as you like]. This is the relationship I have been waiting for.

- I am doing the job [again, be as specific as you like] that I love. I get so much satisfaction and fulfilment from it.

- I live in a beautiful house with a lovely garden. I am so happy here.

Please note that some books tell you to be very specific about your goals and list all your detailed requirements. However, for me, when things were very bad, my main goal was to be happy again and live in a lovely house that was to be my sanctuary. I wasn't at all specific initially as to what the house looked like; I just trusted that the universe would bring to me the right one and it did!

I was, however, specific about my goal for a blue BMW convertible. I wrote my goal down – 'I am driving my beautiful blue 3 series BMW convertible' – and I would visualise myself and my kids driving along with the roof down, the wind blowing through our hair, all happy and smiling.

Do whatever feels right for you. However, I reiterate that you must write your goals down in the present tense as if you have already achieved them and get those feelings going! Indeed, I cannot express the importance and effectiveness of this technique too strongly. Your subconscious mind can only bring this goal to manifestation if it is in the NOW, in the present, in your mind.

Within only a few seconds of focusing your attention and feelings on a subject, you activate the vibration of that subject within you and immediately the law of attraction (see Chapter 3) begins to respond to that activation.

Through the *Teachings of Abraham* (books by Esther and Jerry Hicks), I have learnt that within 17 seconds of focusing on something, a matching vibration becomes activated. Now, as that focus becomes stronger and the vibration becomes clearer, the law of attraction will bring to you more thoughts that match. At this point the vibration will not have much attraction power, but if you maintain your focus longer, the power of the vibration will reach further. If you manage to stay purely focused upon any thought for as little as 68 seconds, the vibration is powerful enough that its manifestation or creation begins.

When you repeatedly return to a pure thought, maintaining it for at least 68 seconds, in a short period of time (hours in some cases or a few days in others), that thought becomes a dominant thought. Once you achieve a dominant thought, you will experience matching manifestations or outcomes until you change that thought.

Research tells us that 80 per cent of people who write down their goals achieve them. Yet it is reckoned that less than 5 per cent of people actually write down their goals and desires.

By writing down your goals, visualising and feeling that success, you are also maintaining focus on your goal, which is crucial.

The importance of maintaining focus

Do you ever focus on something and then find that a load of things related to what you were just thinking about suddenly pop up?

For example, have you ever thought about a particular car and then see that exact same model you were just thinking of, just about everywhere you go? Suddenly they seem to be everywhere!

This happens because you're focused on something particular. The law of attraction and your subconscious mind direct you to the things, people or events related to what you are regularly focused on; your dominant thoughts and goals.

You should know by now that this doesn't happen by chance. These things don't magically pop up. Instead your mind makes a note of what you are focused on. Then, when something related to what you are focused on comes up, your mind quickly notices it.

Your mind is trained to filter out all of the 'junk' that you're not focused on. Your mind will then force you to pay attention to things related to what you are focused on, while ignoring all the stuff that is not related to your focus. How do you make the most of this phenomenon?

- If you want to be in a great relationship – focus on being in a great relationship.

- If you want to make more money – focus on making more money.

- If you want to achieve success – focus on being successful.

Define your success – understand exactly what success means to you. Think of ways in which you can achieve that success and reach your goals. As you do this, your mind will begin to focus on success and it will force you to pay attention to things related to how you define your success.

When this happens, it's important not to get upset, not to get jealous and not to get angry as you notice how others are successful. Remember how different vibrational differences can be! Instead applaud others' success; you'll only attract good things when you encourage others.

Then fine-tune your focus. Get your mind to think about how you can be successful. And once you start doing this you instruct your subconscious mind to pay attention to possibilities for you to be successful. And you instruct your subconscious mind to attract the opportunities for you to be successful.

Get comfortable with success

Whatever your goal is, you have to become comfortable with achieving it. Remember that you deserve it! Begin to believe that achieving your goal will help you improve your life and the lives of those around you.

If you are not comfortable with your goals, if you do not believe that your goals will help you improve your life and the lives of those around you, then you will only attract negative outcomes when you try to achieve your goals.

Here is an example: if you want to be in a loving relationship then get comfortable with the idea of being in a loving relationship. Be entirely comfortable with everything that comes with being in a loving relationship. You can't expect to attract a loving relationship if you believe that you will have to sacrifice too much. You can't expect to be in a loving relationship if you don't believe that there are good men or women out there. Similarly, you can't make millions if you believe that money is the root of all evil.

If you have negative beliefs about achieving your goals, you will only attract situations that will support those negative beliefs. For example, if you believe that relationships require too much sacrifice, you'll only attract people who will force you to make a lot of sacrifices. Also, if you believe that money is the root of all evil, you will only attract people who try to take advantage of you.

When you are comfortable with your goals, when you believe that achieving your goals will improve your life and make you a better person, then your subconscious mind will attract the situations, people and opportunities to achieve your goals.

Belief and trust

The belief and trust that you can and will achieve your goals is crucial to your success. If you don't believe you can achieve your goals, it doesn't matter how hard you try – you just won't get there. If you expect mistakes and failures, it will be a self-fulfilling prophecy.

Successful people believe that they are going to be successful and that they deserve to be successful. If you have any doubt, you have to change your old way of thinking, eliminate negative thoughts (see

Chapter 2) and send new messages to your subconscious mind by way of visualisation (see Chapter 8) and affirmations (see Chapter 10).

If you believe something you trust that what you want can and will happen. Many people I speak to are missing this element in their daily lives. They are prepared to put in the work that is necessary to achieve their goals, but they can't get this element of believing and trusting into their system. There are some people who just can't believe that things will work out for them. They look at past negative results and judge their future on those results. They lose self-esteem and self-confidence and in the end they don't feel like doing very much at all.

The fear of failure and stepping out of one's comfort zone restricts so many people to a life of mediocrity and, so often, misery. But failure doesn't matter – the important thing is to learn from it, let it go and move on. Successful people don't 'do' failure; they call it 'feedback'!

I love the story of Thomas Edison. When he was developing the light bulb he built 10,000 prototypes that did not work before he successfully built the one that we still use today. A reporter asked Edison how it felt to fail 10,000 times. Edison replied, 'You misunderstand. I did not fail at all. I successfully found 10,000 ways that the light bulb would not work.'

Edison did not view failure in the way most other

people do. He viewed it as acceptable and a way to learn and grow.

So how do you get to the required level of belief and trust?

Small steps

First of all you have to get there by taking small steps. Start setting small goals, even with things you know will happen, then trust and believe and see what happens.

You could quite simply do this when you're driving. Trust that you will get to work on time and have an easy drive. Just see what happens after a week of doing this and believing this.

Or if you misplace your keys, for example, tell yourself you know where they are and then trust and believe that you'll find them at the right time. Let go, do something else for a while and see what happens. You'll be amazed at your results!

Three more steps

As your belief and trust grow, so can your goals.

In the meantime, if you're not sure, use these three steps to 'amp up' your belief and expectation and convince yourself that it is possible for you to achieve your goal.

1. **Make a list of other things you have accomplished.** For example, you could list the qualifications you've earned; the project you completed at work; the house you bought; the holiday you took; the lovely children you have; the great meals you cook; the badges you got at school, etc. This exercise will help you get to the feeling, the vibration of success.

2. **Feel a strong desire to attain your goal.** Get excited about it. Strong desire 'amps up' belief and expectation.

3. **Make a list of the reasons why you deserve to attain your goal.** For example, you could list the following: because you want it; because you're a good person; because other people have it, so why not you? Or, because you've wanted it for such a long time. This exercise will raise your belief that you deserve to achieve your goal.

Once belief, trust and expectation are in place, the subconscious mind and the law of attraction will bring into your life the right situations, people and circumstances to help you achieve your goals. These opportunities are like doors opening in life for you, and your route will light up, or they will be presented to you as a flash of inspiration or what I call a 'knowing'.

The most important element here is to act immediately upon opportunities. If you don't walk through the 'door of opportunity' presented to you by the universe, you may lose the moment and delay things further, or worse, lose the opportunity completely.

It took a lot of courage and trust over the years to walk through some doors but how happy I am that I did. I have had and continue to have amazing opportunities to learn and grow.

Nature's timetable

You must also remember to be patient and allow the subconscious mind and the universal laws to get to work. When you are impatient, you will actually push yourself further away from success.

Most people want things yesterday. When people decide they want to achieve something they want it right away and when they decide they want to change or improve, they want that change to happen quickly so that they can begin enjoying their lives and enjoying success.

But we're part of nature and nature doesn't create change in an instant. Therefore, changes within us can't happen instantly. The process can begin instantly, as soon as we take the opportunity – but the change itself cannot.

We're part of nature and we must work with nature and its timetable. Women have been delivering babies since they walked the Earth and it still takes nine months.

When it comes to achieving your goals, your sub-conscious mind, just like nature, has to work through a process and allow you to progressively move closer to achieving your goals.

Philosopher Ralph Waldo Emerson perhaps said it best in one simple line, 'Adopt the pace of nature, her secret is patience.'

Nature works through a process and it has a great deal of patience. An example of this is when you plant a seed, water it, leave it for some time, then at the right time – when all the right elements are in place – that seed turns into an apple tree, a flower, a vege-table or fruit of whatever seed you planted.

This only happens when the conditions are right. But there was work to be done before those elements came into place. The seed had to be planted, it had to be nurtured, it had to be left alone to begin to grow and spring roots under the soil, and then at the right time it began to rise above the surface into exactly what it was meant to be.

Without the prior work of planting and watering,

the seeds would never spring above the ground. If you want to achieve your goals, you have to practise the same kind of patience.

That doesn't mean that you sit around and wait. Instead you have to do the work first, lay the foundation, plant the seed, make sure the soil is right – prepare and then wait for all the elements to come into place before making the right decision that will propel you to greater success.

Unfortunately most people don't practise this process and then one day they realise that they want more out of life, that things just aren't good enough the way they are and that things have to change right away. In the end they feel pressed to make changes immediately only to get frustrated when things don't change instantly.

Instead, think about what you want to achieve, think about the changes you want and begin the process of creating change by knowing what you want and why. Plant your seeds of success in the garden of your mind. Be patient as you watch for signs of progress.

When you're impatient, when you don't trust and accept that things will work out, you actually get slowed down, distracted or end up on the wrong track or giving up – then you wonder, 'How did I get here?'

If you planted a seed and stood over it waiting for

it to sprout through the ground – you'd go crazy before anything happened. If you planted a seed and ignored it – it would die. If you planted a seed and placed a rock on top of it – it would never flourish. But if you planted a seed and did the work to help it grow, cared for it and you were patient, it would flourish and thrive.

Waiting is not patience

But please remember there is a difference between being patient and waiting. I hear people say, 'I've been waiting and waiting for life to improve but it never does. I guess I'll just keep waiting but I'm really tired of this.' Waiting is wasting time. Waiting is not patience.

Waiting in a passive sense is simply wasting time and is not what I mean by being patient. You need to be proactive about doing everything you can to improve your life, but understand that the changes will happen at the right time. You prepare for and trust that the changes will happen. If you merely wait for something to happen but you are not proactive all you are doing is hoping and actually doing very little to improve your life.

Patience requires that you are proactive about doing everything you can to improve your life, while understanding that the changes will happen at the right time. You then prepare for and trust that the changes will happen.

Sometimes, even when we are patient, things don't go according to plan or *our* plan at least! We get 'blocked'. If you keep getting blocked down a particular path, take note! This means this is not the right path or there is something better ahead.

Continue to trust that the right opportunities will come to you, when the time is right.

CHAPTER 10

The Power of Positive Affirmation

Positive affirmations, also referred to as mantras, are an essential part of my powerful mind team in attracting your desired outcomes into your life. Through the consistent use of the simple yet powerful tool of affirmation, combined with creative visualisation (Chapter 8), you will see apparently miraculous changes begin to occur in your life.

We have already learned how affirmations are something that you are doing every minute of every day through your thought process. In fact your consistent and repetitious thoughts *are* affirmations.

Unfortunately, the majority of people in the world today are totally unaware or unconscious as to what those affirmations are. The majority are totally oblivious to the fact that these random thoughts are actually creating the events, conditions and circumstances in their lives whether they are aware of it or not.

As we discovered in Chapter 2, the average human thinks 60,000 thoughts per day. Those thoughts, whether random or focused, conscious or unconscious, represent the seeds that you are planting and are continuously affirming. They consistently feed information to the subconscious mind, which determines what you are attracting and what is manifesting in the form of outcomes that you come to see and experience in your physical world.

Becoming consciously aware

Based on this fact, it is extremely important to develop a conscious and focused affirmation process if you are ever to attain the kind of results that you are seeking. What we will be covering here is becoming consciously aware of exactly what you are affirming through your thoughts. This will enable you purposefully to focus those affirmations on positive and empowering statements, which will attract the results that you desire, instead of unconsciously absorbing and replaying random background noise and attracting those things that you do not want.

You will find that by combining positive affirmations with conscious and focused creative visualisation, you will be overwriting and replacing the random and unconscious thoughts that you may be thinking (unconscious affirmations) with purposeful, focused and powerfully positive affirmations. These will in turn stir up positive and pleasing emotions within you that, through consistency, will begin to attract to you that which you desire. This process is the fastest and most effective way to begin overwriting previously stored data and replacing it with fresh new data that resonates with and will attract to you your 'desired' outcomes and goals.

The importance of positive affirmations cannot be over-emphasised and they are a necessary part of beginning to retrain the subconscious mind. A positive affirmation is a positive present-tense statement that describes a goal in its already completed state and is very much linked to the goal-setting techniques we have already covered in Chapter 9.

A positive affirmation doesn't necessarily have to be a handwritten list of phrases that you go over each day. Other methods can be equally as effective, depending on your preferred mode of receiving and storing information.

Although having a list is the most common

approach to developing the habit of daily positive affirmation, it is not effective for everyone and actually keeps some from ever beginning the process. The most important thing initially is that you begin to recognise when your thoughts are affirming contrary to your desires, and at that moment replace that thought with an empowering and uplifting positive affirmation of your choosing.

The source of your positive affirmation isn't as important as making sure that you are doing it in a way that resonates with you personally. It's worth repeating that the desired outcome results in your positive affirmation stirring the positive emotions within you. If you feel more comfortable establishing your affirmations habit by memory, then do whatever works best for you. The most important thing is that your positive affirmation, whichever form you choose, empowers you and stirs your emotions.

Beginning the process of using positive affirmations

Here, we are going to focus mainly on how to establish and begin a positive affirmation process, which will prove to be most effective for you personally.

Remember, the ultimate goal that will eventually make your positive affirmations noticeably effective is to become conscious of what thoughts are continually running through your mind. By this I mean learning to replace the thoughts that you realise are in opposition with your goals, with positive, focused and creative thoughts that are in alignment with attracting whatever your goals might be.

By developing the habit of using positive affirmations consistently, your subconscious will adapt to the new information it is being provided with and you will begin to overwrite and eliminate the old negative programmes that have become habit and have limited your results up to this point.

In order for affirmations to be 100 per cent effective, it is important that you create your own, based on your individual conditions and circumstances, and gear them specifically to whatever it is that you desire to achieve. It is fine to use prewritten affirmations, but they are only going to be effective if they can ignite your emotions.

It is the emotions that your positive affirmations create that are responsible for attracting the things that you desire, so whichever method you choose to utilise should resonate within you and allow you to feel what it will be like to have whatever it is that your affirmations are being designed to bring into your life.

Choose your method and do it consistently

These are some effective methods for bringing positive affirmations into your life:

- Write out and repeat them

- Memorise and repeat them to yourself

- Use affirmations during meditation (controlled relaxation).

It is important to find the method that fits your particular style and allows you to best connect with the feelings and emotions generated. How you do it is not nearly as important as developing the discipline to make sure that you do it consistently. Indeed, consistency is the key to realising results.

Remember, the whole point behind positive affirmations is to reprogramme or rewrite the subconscious programming that is blocking you from achieving your most sought-after dreams and goals. Doing it consistently will allow the subconscious to absorb the new positive programming that is replacing the negative programming.

The most effective positive affirmations are thoughts or phrases that resonate within you and empower you, allowing you to literally *feel* a shift in your emotions as you speak or think them. If, for example, a thought arises that contradicts your desired outcome and raises the emotion of fear, your positive affirmation should be such that it allows you to experience the opposite. When done correctly and with consistency, you begin to stir the positive emotions attached to them, which allows the subconscious to be penetrated and replaces or rewrites the old self-limiting and negative programming that has been stored there.

The tape recorder explanation

The simplest way to explain this concept is by using the example of a tape recorder. For the sake of the example, let's assume the tape recorder represents your subconscious mind. When you hit the record button and talk into the microphone, the tape recorder doesn't make any judgements as to what is being recorded; it is only doing the job that it was created to do. It is merely recording the data given to it.

The subconscious mind operates in exactly the same way. It only absorbs and records what is being provided to it through the conscious mind and stores the information (or belief) it is given for future use. It uses no rationale to determine what it accepts and makes no judgements as to whether the information is either positive or negative. It merely accepts and records everything that is given to it.

That is why it is extremely important to become conscious of what you are allowing to be recorded through not only your internal thought process but by external means as well, such as the people you associate with, what you watch on TV or read in the newspapers, etc.

By allowing yourself to be bombarded with negativity, regardless of the source, you are literally creating more recordings, which will attract more of the circumstances in your life that you are now working to eliminate.

What you will be accomplishing through the consistent use of positive affirmations is taking the old tapes that you have allowed to be unconsciously recorded and replacing them with focused and conscious positive affirmations (new recordings) that are more in line with what you desire to accomplish.

If, for example, your tape recorder had been accidentally turned on to record mode and left at a busy underground station, you wouldn't expect to be able to hit the play button and listen to your favourite song that you had previously recorded on the tape until you rerecord it. You would only be able to hear the various random background noises that are cre-

ated at a train station. If you have been unconsciously absorbing and recording negative and
self-limiting data, just like the tape recorder, you
can't expect the subconscious to produce specific
and positive results in your life, contrary to the data
it has been given, until you successfully rerecord
new data.

More than likely your subconscious has been
unconsciously absorbing negative and self-limiting
data (random unconscious noise) since you were a
young child, and in order to become a creator of
circumstance, that counterproductive information
(self-limiting beliefs) needs to be replaced.

For instance, if as a child you came to believe that
money was hard to come by, your subconscious mind
is going to react and perform in the way it was
designed to work and make money hard to come by
until you feed it and reprogramme it with the correct
information.

How to phrase your positive affirmations correctly

Let's take a look now at the correct way to phrase
your positive affirmations, so that they are just that,
positive and, even more importantly, effective.

In the present

A correctly structured affirmation should be placed in the present, just as for effective goal setting (see Chapter 9). So, if your intended outcome is becoming financially abundant, your affirmation needs to be structured so that the subconscious understands that it is supposed to be producing it *now*, so that it can begin to immediately act upon it.

A correct way to structure a positive affirmation for financial abundance would be 'I am financially abundant'. If that doesn't feel quite right and is too much of a stretch for you at this point, you could reword it to something along the lines of 'I am allowing myself to be financially abundant'. This may make it easier for you to establish a sincere belief.

On the other hand, if your affirmation was structured like this, 'I am going to have a million pounds', it creates no urgency whatsoever in the subconscious and leaves a lot to chance. 'Going to' could refer to many years down the road!

Tailored to your capabilities

Again, it's important that you tailor your positive affirmation to something that isn't a huge stretch for you. The ability to establish a sincere belief that what you are affirming is really going to happen is extremely important in manifesting whatever it is that you are working towards. If your affirmations are way out there as you begin, it may be difficult for you to ever develop the sincere belief that is necessary.

However, you do need to stretch beyond your current situation if you are going to gain any noticeable results from where you currently find yourself. If you are making £1,200 per month, you may want to tailor your positive affirmation to making £4,000 per month initially, instead of jumping straight to £1,000,000.

Don't allow these instructions to limit you either. Each individual has varying degrees of manifestation capability depending on their individual ability to establish a sincere belief, the depth of previous programming and other factors. For some, results may come very quickly, while for others it may take more time. If you are able to affirm and visualise positively that you have a million pounds in the bank and can actually feel it and clearly see yourself doing those things that having this money allows you to do, regardless of what your current situation is, by all means keep doing it and don't change it!

Remember, it is the initial thought attached to an

emotion produced in the conscious mind that establishes something as belief and stores the information it processes into the subconscious.

Never be negative

It is also imperative that you never structure your positive affirmation in the negative, such as 'I don't want to be poor any more'.

There are actually two reasons for this. By placing your focus on 'not wanting' to be poor you are really focusing your attention on being poor. The subconscious doesn't recognise the negative, 'don't', and only picks up that you want to be poor. Always be sure to structure your affirmations in the positive and place your focus on the intended outcome. In fact, 'want' is a word that you will need to leave out of your positive affirmation, because want implies lack. Replace the word 'want' with 'desire'.

This may seem a minor issue, but it can and will make a difference in the results. By 'wanting' you are actually telling the universe that you want and the universe answers by saying 'OK, here's more want.'

The specific wording and the way that you structure each positive affirmation is extremely important and necessary if you are to have success in attracting your desired outcome. And remember, structuring each positive affirmation in a way that implies the end result has already occurred is also extremely important.

Learn to accept your reality

What you will be accomplishing through consistent and disciplined use of your positive affirmation is taking the false beliefs (old tapes, to use our previous example) that you have absorbed from others or unconsciously recorded and begin replacing them with conscious positive affirmations that are more in line with exactly what you are trying to accomplish.

It is these newly established beliefs, which are stored in the subconscious, that 'kick' in the magnetic law of attraction (Chapter 3), and if you are genuinely *feeling* what it's like to possess what you're affirming, it won't be long until you actually see it! That is exactly the vibratory state that you are trying to achieve.

However, a lot of people struggle with their inner voice telling them not to be stupid as they try to affirm their desires, which appear to be so far from their reality. One thing we must be careful to do is to learn an acceptance of our reality rather than a resistance, before we can truly start affirming positively and effectively for our future.

By learning to develop an acceptance of your current circumstances, regardless of what they might be, you begin to project a specific vibratory output, which emanates at a much higher vibratory rate than resistance. By being in a state of acceptance, it is impossible for the perceived negative event, condition or circumstance to grow! It is against every scientific and spiritual principle. In other words, 'It can't happen'!

Resistance comes from being in a state of fear or lack, and the result is the attraction, manifestation and growth of the thing resisted. Acceptance is derived from acknowledging the circumstances as they are, without fear or feelings of lack, and all that can grow from this state are acceptable or pleasing circumstances.

When you are resisting your current reality, your attention is squarely on what you don't want – your current reality of late bills or old clothes or a rusty car – so you are expanding opportunities to stay stuck. Until we are willing to accept, we remain stuck in our current circumstances. When we accept them, or maybe even thank the universe for the lesson that we are learning here – they change easily enough.

Once we are in a position of accepting reality and not resisting, and have understood that we are 100 per cent responsible (see Chapter 6) for where we are in our lives, we are on an incredibly powerful starting platform for affirming and visualising all that we desire from now on.

Abundance everywhere

Remember, the universe expects us to have abundance and happiness in all areas of our lives, so as you are affirming and visualising consider every aspect. Open your mind up to the possibility of abundance and eliminate those limiting thoughts. In the beginning your mind may refuse to accept the possibility that you can manifest abundance. Your mind will tell you things like, 'It's not possible' or 'That doesn't happen to me.'

If that is the case, just take a look around you and you will see abundance everywhere: the trees, the grass, the air you breathe, etc. There truly is abundance all around you. The universe is continually producing, growing, expanding and thriving in an endless cycle of plenty. Focus on it and you train your mind to accept the possibility of abundance.

Obviously, a positive affirmation doesn't necessarily have to be structured around financial abundance. Whatever it is that you desire to attract can be effectively achieved through this same form of positive affirmation regardless of the intended outcome. Just make certain that whatever the intended outcome it is structured in the now as if it were actually happening.

Use positive affirmations to replace negative thoughts

OK, now that we have a clear understanding of why developing a habit of positive affirmations is so important, let's get into specifically how to construct your positive affirmation in a way that is most effective for you.

There are various ways to do this, depending on your individual circumstances and beliefs. I personally use a few methods that resonate for me. Some of my affirmations are memorised and I sing them, and as I sing and visualise, that stirs the excited emotions within me! Some of my positive affirmations are statements that I say out loud with passion and feeling.

Once you have written or memorised the positive affirmations that you choose to utilise, begin making a focused and conscious effort as you go about your day-to-day activities to become aware of the negative thoughts that surface, those that are contrary to your desired result. When you discover one coming forward, simply stop for a second and replace it with your affirmation.

It is important as you begin your affirmation not to become frustrated or agitated with yourself for having these thoughts as they arise, but instead acknowledge them, thank them for stopping by and replace them with your newly constructed affirmation. You will find that through consistency, the old negative and self-limiting thoughts that you have will eventually and permanently be replaced with your focused positive affirmation.

If this is something new to you, understand that it will take time and some effort on your part to overwrite the previous programming, but the results realised once you have effectively done so will prove to provide far greater rewards than the little effort it took to accomplish it. With a little practice, focused effort and consistency, you will find that your subconscious will begin to absorb and record the new information you are providing it with and your thoughts will naturally and automatically begin to change towards the thing that you are affirming with little to no effort at all. Once this is accomplished, you will begin to experience results that are dramatically different from what you have experienced up to this point.

Health affirmations

Health affirmations can be used in your life in the same way as any other affirmations you might use to help promote wellbeing. Just as you would design affirmations to attract wealth, money or love or anything else, you can tailor affirmations to influence your personal health as well.

After all, what is the good in having everything else in your life if you are not well enough to enjoy it? Though you may be tempted to think that health affirmations are a load of nonsense, you should know that there is solid scientific evidence that supports the use of affirmations and visualisations in the healing process. (I have dedicated Chapter 11 to cover healing and meditation in more detail and I've included some amazing examples.)

Here are some ideas for health affirmations you could use:

- I have the power to control my health and wellbeing.

- I have abundant energy and vitality.

- I am healthy in every aspect of my life.

Some useful general affirmations

Here are a few of the general affirmations I used when I first started reprogramming my subconscious mind all those years ago. They certainly worked for me.

- I trust in the power and the magic of the universe.

- I believe in miracles; miracles happen to me.

- I have more love, happiness and abundance in my life than I ever imagined possible.

- I live so happily in my beautiful home with my happy, safe and confident children.

Wording your affirmations

Here are some examples of the right and wrong way to word your affirmations, remembering to use positive power words in the present tense.

✓ I feel confident and relaxed in any situation.

✗ I am not shy and intimidated by people.

✓ I am action orientated. I enjoy making things happen and getting results.

✗ I am not lazy any more and don't put things off.

✓ I am in a wonderful, loving relationship.

✗ I am not being treated badly by my partner.

In brief, the mechanics you need to concentrate on that make your affirmations powerful are repetition, emotions, consistency, belief and feeling.

Repetition

The importance of repetition cannot be over-emphasised. It imprints the affirmation into your subconscious mind. Research tells us that it can take up to 30 to 40 days of repeated affirmations on a daily basis to reprogramme the subconscious mind.

Emotions

Get involved, be passionate and use your emotions. Think carefully about the meaning of the words as you repeat them, rather than just writing, typing or saying them.

Consistency

If you practise your affirmations with consistency you will achieve results much sooner than if you practise them periodically. Successive sessions will have a compounding effect.

Belief

Don't worry if you don't totally believe your affirmation initially, but keep at it and start to see ways that you can achieve it. Belief will grow with your forthcoming successes.

Feeling

As with goal setting, what you do need is the ability to *feel* what it would be like when the desire you're affirming is fulfilled or your need met. Without this feeling, your affirmation is powerless. The stronger your connection with the affirmation, the deeper the impression it makes on your mind and the sooner you will experience positive results.

How often?

I frequently get asked how often I carry out my affirmations and visualisations each day. I highly recommend doing your affirmations and visualisations one to three times a day, minimum. As we have already seen, the most powerful time to reprogramme the subconscious mind is when you are in alpha state, i.e. when you are in a relaxed state. This is particularly the case when you wake up in the morning and last thing before you fall asleep.

Every night I always make sure I go to sleep with positive affirmations and visualisations. Of course, you should NEVER think about anything that worries you just as you go to sleep.

Any quiet time during the day, maybe driving, instead of listening to music or the radio in the car, I visualise and affirm all my current goals and get very excited about them! You can also do this while you are waiting in a queue or exercising in the gym, etc.

Another option is to record your affirmations and listen to them while you work if you can, or last thing at night as you fall asleep, or you can put Post-it notes around the house with them on. Do whatever works well for you.

Remember the whole powerful mind team!

I have said it before but I cannot stress enough how crucial it is to have all of the members of the powerful mind team working in the same direction for you. Each one on their own will not do the job if all of the others are working in the opposite direction. Remember, all your rowers need to be rowing in the same direction in your life! Go through this checklist:

✓ Accept 100 per cent responsibility for where you are in your life right now.

✓ Let go of past hurts, resentments, bitterness.

✓ Trust in the power of the universal laws and your own mind power.

✓ Think positively and focus on what you have got to be grateful for in life and don't dwell on what is not right. Consciously spend time thinking about what you do want in life and don't think about what you don't want.

✓ Set short-, mid- and long-term goals and bring them into your reality by reprogramming your subconscious mind through use of creative visualisation and affirmations, and eliminate old negative self-limiting beliefs.

The better we feel about ourselves on a daily basis, the more powerful and positive our energy becomes. In Chapter 12 at the end of this book I explore plenty of feel-good techniques that I have learnt over the years. I highly recommend giving the ones that resonate with you a go!

CHAPTER II

Healing and Meditation

The power of thought

The body and mind are intertwined. Every thought, feeling and intention sends ripples throughout your body. The results of these ripples depend upon the nature of your thoughts, feelings and intentions. They can be so powerful that they even affect your genetic code. In his book *It's the Thought That Counts*, scientist Dr David R. Hamilton explains that our bodies are so entangled with the mind that our genes are actually coloured by how we think and feel on a daily basis. Having a particular gene that might produce a disease or protect you from disease, for example, can be switched on and off according to how you process the daily experiences of your life.

The implications of this are enormous. Every function of the human body is susceptible to thoughts and feelings. Scientific studies on DNA have even shown that infants require a mother's loving touch for growth. When this touch is consistently deprived, some of the genes that are responsible for growth simply switch off.

Mind over body

The entire body is hardwired to feel every emotion physically. As it does so, our emotional challenges occasionally show up as physical symptoms in our bodies. Although there are many different causes of cancer, for instance, one factor is the suppression of negative emotion (see Chapter 7). It has been shown that cancers generally progress fastest in people who hold in deep emotional pain, often gathered over many years. The great news is that releasing that pain can halt and even reverse the cancer.

In her life-changing book *The Journey*, Brandon Bays described curing herself of a 'basketball-sized' tumour in her abdomen in six weeks, principally through releasing suppressed negative emotion. She described the process of peeling off the layers of emotion as being similar to peeling an onion. In a demonstration of the link between mind and body, layers of her tumour peeled off too.

We regularly cure aches, pains, illnesses and diseases using our minds, although most of the time we are unaware of what we did. Science has proven that a person who believes he or she is receiving a medicine, although it is really a dummy one – a placebo – will often be cured because of their belief. For instance, in one scientific study patients were given morphine for a serious pain every day for three days, but on the fourth day the morphine was secretly swapped for a placebo – a saltwater solution. Yet the patients still received the pain relief as they did before and even the medical tests recorded the same physiological changes that were recorded when the patient received the morphine. They believed that they were receiving morphine and why wouldn't they? The belief simply neutralised the pain.

The Krebiozen story

Furthermore, here's a story that will challenge your idea of just how much your mind influences your body! It is sourced from an article 'Psychological variables in human cancer' in the *Journal of Projective Techniques*, Vol. 21, No. 4 (December 1957).

In 1950, a new drug called Krebiozen had received

sensational national publicity as a 'cure' for cancer and was being tested by the American Medical Association (AMA) and the US Food and Drug Administration (FDA). One of the researchers involved in this testing was a doctor named Bruno Klopfer.

One of Dr Klopfer's patients, a Mr Wright, was suffering from cancer of the lymph nodes. All standard treatments had been exhausted and Wright appeared to have little time left. His neck, armpits, chest, abdomen and groin were filled with tumours the size of oranges and his spleen and liver were so enlarged that two pints of milky fluid had to be drained out of his body each day.

When Wright discovered that Dr Klopfer was involved in research on Krebiozen, he begged to be given Krebiozen treatments. At first his doctor refused because the drug was untested and only being tried on people with a life expectancy of at least three months. Wright begged so hard, however, that Klopfer decided to give him one injection on Friday, though he secretly suspected Wright would not last the weekend. Dr Klopfer was in for a big surprise.

On the following Monday, Klopfer found Wright out of bed and walking around. Klopfer reported that Wright's tumours had 'melted like snowballs on a hot stove' and were half their original size. This was a far more rapid decrease in size than even the strongest X-ray treatments could have accomplished.

Ten days after Wright's first Krebiozen treatment, he left the hospital with, as far as his doctors could tell, no signs of cancer. When he entered the hospital, he had needed an oxygen mask to breathe, but when he left he was well enough to fly his own plane at 12,000ft with no discomfort.

Wright remained well for about two months, but then articles began to appear asserting that Krebiozen actually had no effect on cancer of the lymph nodes. Wright, who was rigidly logical and scientific in his thinking, became very depressed, suffered relapse and was readmitted to the hospital. This time his physician decided to try an experiment.

Dr Klopfer told Wright that Krebiozen was every bit as effective as it had seemed, but that some of the initial supplies of the drug had deteriorated during shipping. He explained, however, that he had a new, highly concentrated version of the drug and could treat Wright with this. Of course, the physician did not have a new version of the drug and intended to inject Wright with nothing more than plain sterile water. Again the results were dramatic. Tumour masses melted, chest fluid vanished and Wright was quickly back on his feet and feeling great. Yet he had been injected with nothing more than sterile water.

Wright remained symptom-free for another two months, but then the AMA announced that a nation-wide study of Krebiozen had found the drug worthless in the treatment of cancer. This time Wright's faith was completely shattered. His cancer returned and he died shortly after.

Wright's story is tragic, but it contains a powerful message: when we are fortunate enough to bypass our disbelief and tap into the healing forces within each and every one of us, we can truly affect the outcome of our disease.

Psychosomatic illness

The patient's mind alone, independent of the value of the medication, produced his recovery. This event proves that your mind is so powerful that it can literally bring wonderful or tragic events to bear within a very short time. Of course, most people do not learn how to tap into and control this powerful force. In fact, many people do have their minds working for them, but in negative ways. Doctors call this psychosomatic illness – an illness caused by a person's negative belief system.

So, placebo studies clearly show that a belief in wellness results in healing. Some scientists believe this is how visualisation heals. When you visualise and believe in what you are doing, then healing takes place. There are many seemingly miraculous stories of people who have done so.

There's a well-known story of a man who damaged his liver beyond repair in an accident. After spending a while in hospital he was sent home with a contraption that had tubes going into and out of his body. This was for life. But he learnt the technique of creative visualisation and he would spend hours visualising his damaged liver cells being repaired.

At first he saw the cells in his mind as black, shrivelled, damaged prunes. He then took an imaginary toothbrush and imagined cleaning the cells, one by one. As he did this he saw them turn a healthy pink colour.

After three months of visualisation, he had an accident at home and one of the tubes was torn out of his body. He was rushed to hospital and X-rayed to survey the damage prior to an operation. Amazingly, the doctors discovered that his liver was completely repaired!

Ultimately, I don't really think that the actual image we use in visualising is too important. Otherwise, we would all need to use the same ones. The visual image is merely a symbol of what you wish – you intend – to happen. It's the act of keeping your mind on what you wish to happen that's important. The visual image just helps you keep it there.

I may have had my challenges, but thankfully I have never had to overcome a serious health issue. I

have, however, researched and include here some healing techniques using affirmations and visualisation,
which I believe are very effective.

Affirmations for health and wellbeing

We have covered the power of affirmations in
Chapter 10. Here are some further affirmations
specifically aimed at health and wellbeing.

> *Every day in every way, I am getting better*
> *and better [famous quote from Emile*
> *Coué]*
> *I have all the energy required for my needs*
> *The light within me is healing my entire body*
> *Divine light flows through every cell of my*
> *body*
> *I sleep relaxed and awake refreshed*
> *I am in control of my health and wellbeing*
> *I have abundant energy, vitality and*
> *wellbeing*
> *I am healthy in all areas of my life*
> *I am able to maintain my ideal weight*
> *I am calm; my mind and body is at peace*
> *I love and care for my body*
> *I am perfect just the way I am.*

Visualisation and healing

Visualisation is a tool used to fight cancer. Its effectiveness will vary from individual to individual. One
of the reasons why cancer is able to grow is because
the immune system has not been able to recognise the
cancer. For this reason, cancer is more difficult to
knock out with visualisation than the common cold.
That doesn't mean that visualisation can't work with
cancer. It just means that it doesn't work for everyone. However, all cancer patients should practise
visualisation. Visualisation can be the trick that
wakes up your immune system to recognise the
cancer.

There are three common types of visualisation: the
healing process, the healing partner and the healthy
body. For any of these to be effective, it is important
to be in a relaxed or meditative state and it is a good
idea to practise the following exercise before entering
into any of the visualisations.

First, find a quiet place in which you can practise your visualisation. Start by imagining yourself in a safe and peaceful
place. Then begin relaxing your entire body. Relax the top of
your head, then your face muscles. Progressively work your
way through your entire body, concentrating on relaxing

each part, from your arms to your hands, to your stomach, to your legs, to your feet. After your body is completely relaxed, you can undertake one of the following visualisation exercises. Some people combine elements from each of these exercises.

The healing process

The healing process is one of the most common visualisation methods. It involves picturing your immune system taking care of the cancer cells. The images you use for your immune system and the cancer can be almost anything. There is no evidence that realistically picturing your immune system attacking the cancer is any more effective than picturing a metaphorical attack on the cancer. A metaphorical visualisation effort might see the immune cells as knights and the cancer cells as dragons. A realistic visualisation exercise might see the killer T cells of the immune system as a blur attacking the cancer cells within the bone marrow and bloodstream. You might then see the dead cancer cells being carried through the bloodstream by macrophage cells to the kidney and the spleen. Another realistic visualisation exercise might imagine enzymes repairing broken DNA.

The healing partner

With this method, after relaxing the entire body, imagine that a healing partner has joined you. The partner could be Jesus, Buddha, your spirit guide, an imaginary friend, an animal, a ball of light – anything you desire. Your healing partner is someone you can trust to help you. Ask your healing partner questions for which you are seeking answers on how to heal. Ask your healing partner to come into your body and help you heal. Imagine your healing partner being there for you to guide you through the entire healing process.

The healthy body

This visualisation exercise involves picturing your body in its highest form of health. Imagine your body as perfect and fully capable of healing from any illness. To facilitate the visualisation of your perfect body, you might imagine that it is enveloped by and even absorbing a bright white light or see your body radiating with golden light. See each cell of your body singing and vibrating with this intense light. See your body as a shimmering mass of joyous, balanced energy. Nothing can impede this vibration: you are flowing and in total balance. Project the future and 'see' yourself whole and healed.

Metaphors for visualisations

Here are some metaphors to use for healing visualisations:

Rebuilding a collapsed wall
Putting a jigsaw puzzle together

Knitting tissue with needles and yarn
Seeing new, healthy cells multiply
Divine healing energy as golden light
Seeing the actual body areas mending, clearing
*   and healing*

These metaphors are useful for pain relief:

A vice loosening, then disintegrating
Ropes untying
Flames dying out from a cool wind
Cool colours such as green, blue and violet
*   replacing hot colours like red and orange*
A taut rubber band loosening

Try to visualise for 10 to 20 minutes per session, working up to three times a day: in the early morning, late afternoon and at bedtime.

Further investigations into healing and meditation

Warning: The remainder of this chapter isn't going to be for everyone!

I am a very practical, level-headed and grounded person and during my journey of transformation I have become very aware of the spiritual side of life. Personally, over the years I have had enough evidence that now I do not question its existence and have found it to be wonderfully empowering in every way.

For the last few years I have been running and organising the Positive Living Group of Bournemouth (www.powerofpositiveliving.com). This group is for anyone who wants to learn about alternative healing therapies, spiritual awareness and the bigger picture of life. Each week we have a different speaker talking and demonstrating on a great variety of subjects, and my own awareness of the various types of alternative healing therapies has expanded enormously.

I want to share with you what I consider to be one of my healing 'miracles', following a horse riding accident I had in September 2005.

I was in the lane outside my house on my horse Alabama, when the dustman collecting our rubbish frightened her. She reared up, lost her footing and crashed back into the road, directly onto the tarmac and deposited me on the roadside beside her. I was lucky she did not land on me, but I was in an awful lot of pain and an ambulance was called as we thought I had broken my hip and my elbow. Luckily Alabama was fine, just a bit shaken, as of course I was!

Once in hospital and after a few X-rays, it became apparent that nothing was broken. I was very relieved but still suffering from excruciating pain and could not bear any weight. Every time I tried to get going on the crutches they gave me I passed out, partially also due to low blood pressure. Much to the relief of my children, the hospital decided to keep me in overnight.

The following day I went home and coped fairly well on the crutches and, very sweetly, the dustman came round with a box of chocolates to make sure I was OK!

The hospital told me that the physiotherapy department would be in touch, but probably not for a couple of weeks.

The next Monday was our Positive Living night and I went along, still on crutches and unable to bear any weight, and Natalie, Richard and Nick came along to do all the work for me. Two of the healers, Ivan and Sue, said: 'Sue, your body is out of alignment after your accident; no wonder you can't walk, we are coming round to sort you out on Wednesday!'

And indeed they did! They worked on me for approximately one and a half hours, doing reflexology and reiki healing. For anyone who does not know, very simply and briefly, reflexology is a holistic treatment and involves the application of pressure, stretch and movement to the feet and hands to affect corresponding parts of the body. Reiki healing is a hands-on therapy that gently balances life energies and brings health and wellbeing to the recipient.

It truly was a mini miracle for me. When they

arrived I could barely put my leg down but by the time they had finished I was walking around the room completely normally, unaided and pain free! Quite honestly, my children and I were 'blown away' by the effects of the treatment. It had also been a most relaxing and calming experience, involving no painful manipulation whatsoever.

There are so many types of alternative healing therapies and I could not possibly begin to mention them all here, but I have witnessed some amazing results myself and seen them in others. From experience I've seen how different healing methods resonate with different people. It is always best to see someone who has been personally recommended to you and if it 'feels' right to you then it most probably is right for you! Health food shops and New Age shops, etc. all carry leaflets and cards from therapists too.

Spiritual healing

I've met and continue to meet spiritual/energy healers, many of whom truly do a wonderful job in helping remove those deep-rooted blocks! There are too many to mention here but there is one in particular I would like to share with you.

His name is Wayne Lee and he calls himself a 'spirit surgeon' and I have been very impressed with the results that he is getting. Already operating as a psychic and trance medium, he explained to me how one day he was approached during a trance medium session by a spirit doctor who introduced himself as his 'medical controller' by the name of Selwyn Brieght. Selwyn Brieght told him that there were up to 14 spirit doctors and surgeons who were waiting to work with him and he needed to start to do spirit surgery.

Wayne explained that spirit surgery is simply spirit surgeons taking over his body, so they can use his energy to work both on and inside the client's body and energy fields. They can do some of the most incredible work without doing any damage to the existing body tissue. He said that he asks the spirit doctors to explain what they are doing so he can understand it. He feels that the more he understands the more effective it is, as his mind does not block their work.

Wayne strongly believes that healers are often misunderstood, with many people thinking they are capable of healing anyone. He told me that being a healer is not what many people think it is. Healers are not able to heal just anyone as the healing process can only be done by the person who is in need of healing, so in reality you can only heal yourself. But you can get help with your healing and that is where healers come in. However, healing should be done for the highest of good beyond the healer's understanding.

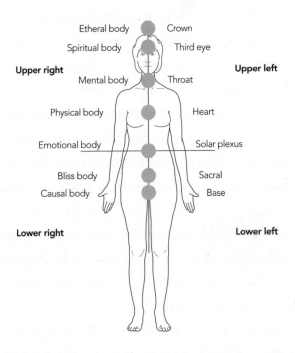

Upper right

Etheral body   Crown
Spiritual body   Third eye
Mental body   Throat
Physical body   Heart
Emotional body   Solar plexus
Bliss body   Sacral
Causal body   Base

Upper left

Lower right   Lower left

Wayne went on to explain to me how he sees the human form from a healer's perspective. It is very important to understand that we do not only have one body; we have seven bodies (which includes our physical body) and each of these bodies is connected to a chakra or energy centre (see illustration). A chakra is the communication crossroad between our seven bodies.

He continued to explain to me that if one of the chakras is not working properly, this can affect our day-to-day lives and cause physical pains or mental worries. For instance, if you are a person who does not always speak up, this would suggest that your throat chakra is not functioning correctly. This often causes headaches, anxiety, anger or depression, as the flow of energy coming down through your crown chakra is unable to flow through your body, creating more energy pressure within the head and causing stress or anxiety. Once the chakra has been un-blocked the energy can flow more easily through the body and once again bring the body back to its normal self.

Wayne also told me that the solar plexus chakra is the chakra that is most important in healing of the physical body. This is due to the fact that not only is it the seat of our emotions, it is also the place in our body where our 'chi' is stored. Chi is the energy our body uses, similar to our own battery. If the solar plexus chakra is not functioning correctly then it causes an imbalance between all four quadrants of the body.

I have found it amazing how quickly Wayne gets results. He described to me how he finds that when opening up and cleansing the solar plexus chakra there is often a very quick and profound change to the client's wellbeing and self-balance.

In order to heal, Wayne places his hands on his patient and the healing is very powerful and seem-ingly miraculous! The spirit doctors and surgeons who work with and through him are concerned mainly with the cause of illness, blockage or pain.

The pain is easily dealt with but if they do not focus on the cause of the pain then the pain, blockage or illness can very easily be remanifested and the cycle begins again. So to assist people with this problem they work with a process called neuro pathway regeneration (NPR), which he explained to me as the clearing of old thought pathways in the brain. An old thought pathway is, for example, when a person believes that they need to eat to make themselves feel happy and thus find themselves overeating. If they want to change this pattern and are progressively trying to do so, a NPR treatment will assist them. In this instance, NPR will be in the form of clearing their thought pathway and allowing them to create new, more constructive pathways. The brain will then regenerate a healthier pathway and thus rid the body of old habits.

Wayne told me how important he believes it is for the recipient to want to and be ready to make the change, as the body will easily reform the old pathway it had before. Some people grow out of the habit without changing the neuro pathway, so after a NPR treatment they find it natural to move forward and create the space for a more open and happier pathway.

He told me that it is important to remember that the regeneration does not make the change happen, but that it is merely a method of cleaning the slate of pathways that affect our choices, healing pathways and programming. It remains up to the patient to create the desired pathways they feel will change their lives and make them happier.

When a person has an illness, NPR assists by clearing or increasing the flow of energy going through the brain and targets the most important areas to do with healing with that illness. Our brain is the central processing unit in our bodies and thus even small changes can create big results.

It's been fascinating to find out more from the many healers I have come across. I have learnt so much and I hope you have found this chapter on healing and meditation enlightening too. I urge you to carry on exploring along this path; there are many resources and further information available in books and on the internet.

CHAPTER 12

Feeling Good

Feeling good about yourself helps you exude an extremely positive vibration and you should know by now what that means! Feeling good about yourself helps you feel happier and healthier.

We have already covered in great depth the importance of choosing positive thoughts and feelings and having an 'attitude of gratitude'. In addition, I've always believed in giving everything my best shot; this can minimise or eliminate any feelings of regret, leaving one with a sense of peace and calm whatever the outcome.

In this concluding chapter I thought I would share with you some more of the 'feel good' techniques and tips I have learnt and practised over the years.

An enthusiastic approach

A great starting point is to adopt an enthusiastic approach to life, each and every day! Always anticipate exciting fun things happening in your life. I always do and guess what? Exciting fun things are always happening to me! Do you ever wake up in the morning and all you want to do is bury yourself in bed and not face the day? Several years ago that thought went through my mind on a regular basis.

Here is a great technique I learnt from Zig Ziglar's book *See You at the Top*. It will help you overcome that feeling and set you up for the day. It sounds a bit silly, but try it; I promise you it works!

Sit on the edge of your bed and clap your hands together several times and say out loud something along the lines of 'Goodie, goodie, goodie what exciting things has the universe in store for me today?' Say it with feeling and excitement if you can. You will probably laugh at yourself (and your partner if you do it together!). This will immediately change your mood and indeed your energetic vibration for the day. If you *believe* you are going to have a bad day and things are going to go wrong, the chances are this will probably happen!

Chanting a powerful affirmation, such as 'I'm feeling great today', as you are getting ready in the morning also works for me. Say it several times, even sing it, but try and say it as if you mean it and it will send a surge of vitality and energy throughout your body.

Smile!

I love to smile! It is so simple. A smile is more than just a look – it's a feeling, it's a trigger for happiness and inner peace. Most of us do not appreciate that when we smile or laugh, our body releases endorphins (those pain-killing hormones that make us feel good), which in turn make us happy or at least happier.

Smiling is contagious. Not only is smiling good for us but also if you find a friend having one of those rainy or down days, smiling and trying to make them smile and laugh is possibly the greatest thing you could do for them. When you are feeling stressed, whether it's that big meeting coming up or just a build-up of the stresses of everyday life, the best medicine is a smile. So, if you've lost your sense of humour, the best thing is to find it again immediately. When we laugh or smile the released endorphins trigger a reduction in our stress hormone levels.

Babies are actually born with the emotional makeup to smile when feeling pleasure. So smiling is not a response taught to us from life experiences but rather a natural sign of pleasure or delight.

We were born to smile. A smile is worth more than words. A smile is a universal language expressed in the form of a gesture that greets and welcomes other people. When someone smiles at you, especially at a time you least expect it, you feel happier and you return the favour. A smile is contagious and has no monetary value yet it is priceless.

I know it is hard to smile when you are overwhelmed with problems. But does sulking help? Will a frown take away the pain and rid you of the problems that keep you down? The answer is obvious. Without a shadow of a doubt, a smile will clear the clouds and bring a little sunshine into your life.

Be kind to others, and to yourself

Being kind is so important and makes us feel good. Kindness is a generosity of spirit. It comes to life when we give of our time and ourselves to be of help to others, without expecting anything in return. When you show kindness to somebody you bring out the best in yourself and a side effect of brightening up somebody else's day is to feel happier in the moment yourself.

Pay attention to the impact your behaviour has on others and notice your own feelings in response to their reactions. Think about how you feel yourself when somebody else shows you kindness. What you give comes back to you in even greater quantity. When you are kind you not only get an immediate payback in terms of a feel good factor, you will also receive kindness from others and in completely unexpected and unrelated ways.

It is so easy to find ways to be kind to others: say something supportive when you instinctively feel someone needs to hear it; offer help without being asked for it; smile encouragingly; swallow your criticisms; listen without judgement; let mistakes slide instead of assigning blame; make small sacrifices for the benefit of somebody in greater need.

A great rule of thumb I try and apply to my life is 'to do unto others as I'd have them do unto me' and 'do unto myself as I'd do unto others'. The latter part is just as important as the first. It is no good being consistently kind to others and forgetting to be kind to yourself. You will run out of steam and feel less able to show kindness to others if you don't replenish your own mind, body and spirit on a regular basis.

Being kind to yourself means getting your needs met, being gentle with yourself instead of critical when you feel you're not performing at your best, forgiving yourself when the need arises instead of beating your-self up. When you get into the habit of treating yourself with kindness, it becomes much easier to extend that consideration and behaviour to others.

Other tips for feeling good

Boost your energy

Boost your energy, as studies show that when you are feeling energetic, you're much more likely to feel good about yourself. For a quick shot of energy, take a brisk ten-minute walk (outside if possible where sun-light will also stimulate your brain) or if that is not possible, listen to some great music or chat with a positive, upbeat friend. I love going outside to 'poo pick' the paddock where the horses have been. It is good exercise, wonderfully 'grounding' and makes me feel great!

Do a good deed

How about doing a good deed for someone? This is, in the nicest possible way, as selfish as it is selfless; you'll benefit as much as the person you are helping.

When you are feeling low, thinking about the time you helped someone will make you feel much better than recalling every compliment you have ever received!

Keep a resolution

Keeping a resolution gives a great feeling of satisfaction. Not only will you benefit from clearing out your garage or cupboard, for example, you will also get a boost from the mere fact that you made a commitment to yourself and you stuck to it.

Master something new

How about taking up a new hobby or becoming an expert? There is great satisfaction in mastery. Pick a subject that interests you and spend time researching it. It could be anything from a period in history to wine tasting! This is also a great way of boosting your self-confidence.

You *are* capable of doing *anything* you put your mind to! Open your mind to all possibilities and truly you will find the sky is the limit!

Release the hidden power of your subconscious mind

You CAN bring into your life more happiness, better health and more wealth by using your thoughts and feelings to contact and release the hidden power of your subconscious mind.

> Remember, you do not need to acquire this power; you already have it within you.

Your subconscious mind is all-wise and knows the answers to all questions, but it won't argue with you or talk back to you. So when you say, 'I can't do this', 'I am too old now', 'I haven't got enough money', 'I'm no good at that', you are impregnating your subconscious mind with these negative thoughts and it *does* respond accordingly.

You are actually blocking your own good and bringing lack, limitation and frustration into your life. The unwavering powers of the universal laws will see to that!

We must understand that our mind is an amazing instrument and we must use it with care. Consider the following:

- Negative thinking creates negative results

- Mediocre thinking creates mediocre results

- Great thinking creates great results!

There are two things that we have complete control over in our lives:

Number 1: What we think

Number 2: Our attitude to life

Whatever thought has done in your life so far, don't worry. Just by having a shift in your awareness and thought process you can start creating the life you dream of.

I've turned my life around and I've helped others turn theirs around too. Now it's your turn. Start today, if you haven't already. If I can do it, so can you.

Good luck and get going!

Recommended Reading

The following are some books that you may find useful in furthering your knowledge and understanding of some of the concepts in this book.

Brandon Bays (1999) *The Journey*, Thorsons

Jack Canfield (2005) *The Success Principles*, Element Books

Diana Cooper (2004) *A Little Light on the Spiritual Laws*, Mobius

Diana Cooper (2008) *Angel Answers*, Hodder Paperbacks

Diana Cooper (1995) *Light Up Your Life*, Piatkus

Wayne W. Dyer (2007) *Change Your Thoughts, Change Your Life*, Hay House

Gill Edwards (2006) *Stepping Into the Magic*, Piatkus

The Dalai Lama and Howard C. Cutler (1999) *The Art of Happiness*, Mobius

Dr David R. Hamilton (2007) *Destiny vs Free Will*, Hay House

Dr David R. Hamilton (2008) *How Your Mind Can Heal Your Body*, Hay House

Dr David R. Hamilton (2008) *It's the Thought That Counts*, Hay House

Louise L. Hay (2004) *You Can Heal Your Life*, Hay House

Ester Hicks and Jerry Hicks (2005) *Ask and It Is Given*, Hay House

Napoleon Hill (2008) *Think and Grow Rich*, Wilder Publications

Anne Jones (2002) *Heal Yourself*, Piatkus

Anne Jones (2003) *The Ripple Effect*, Piatkus

Anne Jones (2002) *Healing Negative Energies*, Piatkus

Anne Jones (2007) *Opening Your Heart*, Piatkus

Anne Jones (2008) *The Soul Connection*, Piatkus

Byron Katie (2002) *Loving What Is*, Rider & Co.

Paul McKenna (2004) *Change Your Life in 7 Days*, Bantam Press

Ian Lawton (2008) *The Big Book of the Soul*, Rational Spirituality Press

Dr Joseph Murphy (2008) *The Power of Your Subconscious Mind*, Wilder Publications

Anthony Robbins (2001) *Awaken the Giant Within*, Pocket Books

Sanaya Roman (1989) *Spiritual Growth*, H. J. Kramer

Dr Helen Wambach (1982) *Life Before Life*, Bantam Press

Zig Ziglar (2000) *See You at the Top*, Pelican

Index